Janice VanCleave's

A+
PROJECTS IN
PHYSICS

Janice VanCleave's

A+
PROJECTS IN
PHYSICS

Winning Experiments for
Science Fairs and Extra Credit

WILEY

John Wiley & Sons, Inc.

Dedication

It is my pleasure to dedicate this book to a very knowledgeable and talented teacher, who has patiently provided me with answers to my many questions about physics. This valuable information has made this book even more understandable and fun. It has been an honor to work with such an esteemed colleague, the head of the department of physics at Texas A&M University–Commerce in Commerce, Texas:

Dr. Ben Doughty

Acknowledgments

I wish to express my appreciation to these science specialists for their valuable assistance by providing information and/or assisting me in finding it.

Holly Harris, Dr. Tineke Sexton, and Robert Fanick. Holly Harris is a science teacher in China Spring, Texas. She not only helped with the research for the book but was one of the technical reviewers. Dr. Sexton is an instructor of biology and microbiology at Houston Community College Northwest–Houston, Texas, and Robert Fanick is a chemist at Southwest Research Institute in San Antonio, Texas.

Members of the Central Texas Astronomical Society, including Johnny Barton, Dick Campbell, John W. McAnally, and Paul Derrick. Johnny is an officer of the club and has been an active amateur astronomer for more than 20 years. Dick is an amateur astronomer who is interested in science education. John is also on the staff of The Association of Lunar and Planetary Observers, where he is acting Assistant Coordinator for Transmit Timings of the Jupiter Section. Paul is the author of the "Stargazer" column in the *Waco Tribune-Herald*.

Dr. Glenn S. Orion, a Senior Research Scientist at the Jet Propulsion Laboratory of California Institute of Technology. Glenn is an astronomer and space scientist who specializes in investigating the structure and composition of planetary atmospheres. He is best known for his research on Jupiter and Saturn. I have enjoyed exchanging ideas with Glenn about astronomy facts and experiments for modeling astronomy experiments.

A special note of gratitude to these educators who assisted by pretesting the activities and/or by providing scientific information: Anne Skrabanek, homeschooling consultant, Perry, Texas; Connie Chatmas, Sue Dunham, and Stella Cathey, consultants, Marlin, Texas.

Contents

Part IV   Heat

Part V   Light

Part VI   Sound

Part VII   Measurement

Introduction

Science is a search for answers to all kinds of interesting questions about our world. Science projects make excellent tools for you to use as you look for the answers to specific problems. This book will give you guidance and provide A+ project ideas. An A+ idea is not a guarantee that you will receive an A+ on your project. You must do your part by planning experiments, finding and recording information related to a problem, and organizing the data to find the answer.

Sharing your findings by presenting your project at science fairs will be a rewarding experience if you have properly prepared the exhibit. Trying to assemble a project overnight usually results in frustration, and you cheat yourself out of the fun of being a science detective. Solving a scientific mystery, like solving a detective mystery, requires that you plan well and carefully collect facts.

Start your project with curiosity and a desire to learn something new. Then proceed with purpose and a determination to solve the problem. It is likely that your scientific quest will end with some interesting answers.

Select a Topic

The 30 topics in this book suggest many possible problems to solve. Each topic has one "cookbook" experiment—follow the recipe, and the result is guaranteed. Read all of these easy experiments before choosing the topic you like best and want to know more about. Regardless of the problem you choose to solve, your discoveries will make you more knowledgeable about physics.

Each of the 30 sample projects begins with a brief summary of topics to be studied and objectives to be determined. Information relevant to the project is also included in the opening summary. Terms are defined when first used in the project, but definitions are not repeated throughout the text. Check the Glossary and/or Index to find explanations about any unfamiliar terms.

Try New Approaches

Following each of the 30 introductory experiments is a section titled "Try New Approaches," which provides additional questions about the problem presented. By making small changes to some part of the sample experiment, you achieve new results. Think about why these new results might have happened.

Design Your Own Experiment

In each chapter, the section titled "Design Your Own Experiment" allows you to create experiments to solve questions related to the sample problem. Your own experiment should follow the sample experiment's format and include a single statement of purpose; a list of necessary materials; a detailed step-by-step procedure; written results with diagrams, graphs, and charts, if they seem helpful; and a conclusion explaining why you got the results you did and answering the questions you posed to yourself. To clarify your answer, include any information you found through research. When you design your own experiment, make sure to get adult approval if supplies or procedures other than those given in this book are used.

Get the Facts

Read about your topic in many books and magazines. You are more likely to have a successful project if you are well informed about the topic. For each topic in this book, the section titled "Get the Facts" provides some tips to guide you to specific sources of information. Keep a journal to record all the information you find from each source, including the author's name, the title of the book or article, the page numbers, the publisher's name, the city of publication, and the year of publication.

Keep a Journal

Purchase a bound notebook to serve as your journal. Write in it everything relating to the project. It should contain your original ideas as well as ideas you get from books or from people such as teachers and scientists. It should also include descriptions of your experiments as well as diagrams, photographs, and written observations of all your results.

Every entry should be as neat as possible and dated. An orderly journal provides a complete and accurate record of your project from start to finish and can be used to write your project report. It is also proof of the time you spent sleuthing out the answers to the scientific mystery you undertook to solve, and you will want to display the journal with your completed project.

Use the Scientific Method

Each project idea in this book will provide foundation material to guide you in planning what could be a prize-winning project. With your topic in mind and some background information, you are ready to demonstrate a scientific principle or to solve a scientific problem via the **scientific method.** This method of scientifically finding answers involves the following steps: research, purpose, hypothesis, experimentation, and conclusion.

Research: The process of collecting information about the topic being studied. It is listed as a first step because some research must be done first to formulate the purpose and hypothesis. Additional research will help you explain your experimental results.

Purpose: A statement that expresses the problem or question for which you are seeking resolution. Once you have settled on an idea you want to investigate, turn it into a clear purpose statement.

Hypothesis: A guess about the answer to the problem based on knowledge and research you have done before beginning the project. It is most important to write down your hypothesis before beginning the project and not to change it even if experimentation proves you wrong.

Experimentation: The process of testing your hypothesis. Safety is of utmost importance. The projects in this book are designed to encourage you to learn more about physics by altering a known procedure, but please explore untested materials or procedures only with adult supervision or approval.

Conclusion: A summary of the experimental results and a statement that addresses how the results relate to the purpose of the experiment. Include explanations for experimental results that support or refute the hypothesis.

Assemble the Display

Keep in mind that while your display represents all that you have done, it must tell the story of the project in such a way that it attracts and holds the viewer's interest. So keep it simple. Try not to cram all your information into one place. To conserve space on the display and still exhibit all your work, keep some of the charts, graphs, pictures, and other materials in your journal instead of on the display board itself.

The actual size and shape of displays vary according to local science fair official rules. Remember to check them out for your particular fair. Most exhibits are allowed to be 48 inches (122 cm) wide, 30 inches (76 cm) deep, and 108 inches (274 cm) high. Your display may be smaller than these maximum measurements. A three-sided backboard (see Figure I.1) is usually the best way to display your work. A cardboard or foam backboard can be purchased, or wooden panels can be hinged together, but you can also use sturdy cardboard pieces taped together to form a very inexpensive, but presentable, exhibit.

Your title should be placed at the top of the center panel. The title should be as short as possible and capture the theme of the project but not be the same as the problem statement. For example, suppose the problem under question is "How does weight affect the period of a pendulum?" An effective title might be "Back and Forth: Timing a Harmonic Oscillator." The title and other headings should be neat and also large enough to be readable from a distance of about 3 feet (1 m). You can glue letters onto the backboard (buy precut letters or cut them out of construction paper), or use a computer to create them for all the titles. A short summary paragraph of about 100 words to explain the scientific principles involved is useful and can be printed under the title. Someone

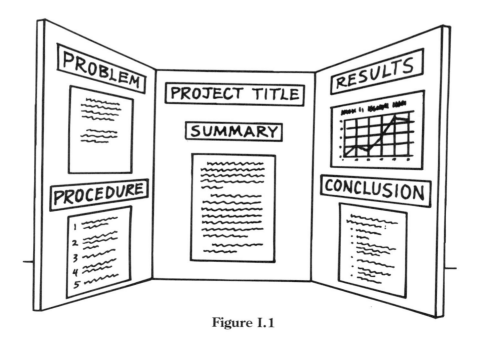

Figure I.1

who has no knowledge of the topic should be able to easily understand the basic idea of the project just by reading the summary.

There are no set rules about the position of the information on the display. However, it all needs to be well organized, with the title and summary paragraph as the focal point at the top of the center panel and the remaining material placed neatly from left to right under specific headings. The headings you display will depend on how you wish to organize the information. Separate headings of "Problem," "Procedure," "Results," and "Conclusion" may be used.

Discuss the Project

The judges give points for how clearly you are able to discuss the project and explain its purpose, procedure, results, and conclusion. While the display should be organized so that it explains everything, your ability to discuss your project and answer the questions of the judges convinces them that you did the work and understand what you have done. Practice a speech in front of friends, and invite them to ask you questions. If you do not know the answer to a question, never guess or make up an answer or just say "I do not know." Instead, say that you did not discover that answer during your research, and then offer other information that you found of interest about the project. Be proud of the project, and approach the judges with enthusiasm about your work.

PART I

Force and Motion

Center of Gravity: The Balancing Point

Any object can be balanced if it is supported at the right place. This place is at or in line with a point called the center of gravity.

In this project, you will discover how to locate the center of gravity of a symmetrical (having matching halves) space figure (geometric figure that is three-dimensional) with uniform density (mass per volume) as well as of an irregularly shaped object with an irregular density. You will also find the center of gravity of a plane figure (a geometric figure that lies flat on a surface). You will then investigate how the height of an object's center of gravity and the width of an object's base affect the object's mechanical stability (how easily it falls over).

Getting Started

Purpose: To find the center of gravity of a symmetrical space figure with uniform density.

Materials
18-inch (45-cm) piece of string
⅜-by-36-inch (1-by-90-cm) dowel
transparent tape
marker
yardstick (meterstick)

Procedure
1. Tie one end of the string around the dowel.
2. Tape the free end of the string to the edge of a table. The dowel should hang freely.
3. Move the dowel through the loop of string until it balances while hanging in a horizontal position.
4. Mark the position of the string on the dowel.
5. Use the yardstick (meterstick) to measure the distance to the mark from each end of the dowel.

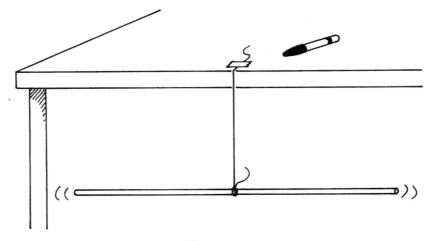

Figure 1.1

Results

Your measurements will show that the mark is at the center of the dowel. The dowel balances when supported at this mark.

Why?

The place on a **space figure** (geometric figure that is three-dimensional), such as the dowel, where it can be balanced is in line with a point called its **center of gravity** (point where the weight of an object appears to be concentrated). If the space figure is perfectly **symmetrical** (having matching halves) on either side of the center of gravity and its density (mass per volume) is **uniform** (the same throughout; unchanging), then the balancing point is in the geometric center, as you found in your experiment. Note that **mass** is the amount of **matter** (substance of which physical objects consist) in an object.

    A **force** is a push or a pull on an object. **Gravity** is the force of attraction between all objects in the universe. **Weight** is the measure of the force of gravity, which on Earth is a measure of the force with which Earth's gravity pulls an object toward Earth's center. The dowel is made of many particles, each having weight. Figure 1.2 diagrams a few of the weight **vectors** (quantities with directions that are expressed by arrows). The position of the string is shown by the large arrow F. The string supports the dowel with a force equal to the sum of all the weights of the particles. In addition, each of the particles exerts a rotating effect,

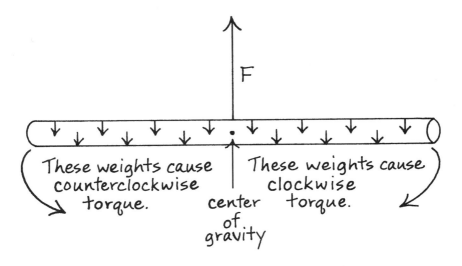

Figure 1.2

called torque, because of its weight and position. **Torque** is the product of a force and its perpendicular distance from a point about which it causes rotation. **Rotation** is the turning motion of an object about its **axis** (imaginary line through the center of an object and around which the object turns). Because the dowel is supported at one point, the torques of the particles on one side of the support rotate the dowel clockwise, and the torques of the particles on the opposite side of the support rotate the dowel counterclockwise. The dowel balances when the string is placed at the point around which the sum of the clockwise torques equals the sum of the counterclockwise torques. The string is above the center of gravity. When an object is supported by a single force, the force goes through the center of gravity of the object.

Try New Approaches

1a. Where is the center of gravity if the object is not symmetrical with uniform density? Repeat the experiment placing a weight, such as a walnut-size piece of modeling clay, on one end of the dowel. Where is the center of gravity in relation to the added weight?

b. Repeat the investigation, placing the weight at different points along the dowel.

Science Fair Hint: Make display diagrams for each investigation similar to the one in Figure 1.2.

Design Your Own Experiment

1. If an object is supported at any point other than at or in line with its center of gravity, unbalanced torque on either side of the center of gravity causes the object to rotate about the support until its center of gravity is as low as possible. Design a way to demonstrate how this fact makes it possible to find the center of gravity of a **plane figure** (a geometric figure that lies on a flat surface) with an irregular shape. One way is to cut an irregular shape from a stiff piece of thin cardboard (see Figure 1.3). Use a one-hole paper punch to cut four or more holes around the edge of the cardboard. Hang the cardboard on a tackboard by inserting a pushpin through one of the holes. Make sure the figure can swing freely on the pin. Cut a piece

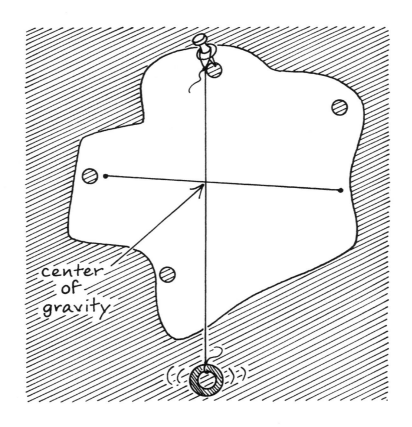

center
of
gravity

Figure 1.3

of string slightly longer than the widest part of the cardboard. Tie a weight, such as a metal washer, to one end of the string and make a loop in the other end large enough to slip over the head of the push-pin. While the cardboard is suspended by the pin, slip the loop of the string over the pin's head and allow the string to hang freely. The string should almost touch the cardboard. Mark two points on the cardboard under the string, one near the hole and the other near the edge of the cardboard (see Figure 1.3). Take the cardboard down and draw a line between the two points. Repeat the procedure using the other holes in the cardboard. The lines overlap on the center of gravity.

2a. The measure of the ability of an object to resist falling over is known as its **mechanical stability.** How does the relationship between the height of the center of gravity of an object and the height of the object affect its mechanical stability? Design a way to measure the effect of a high or low center of gravity on mechanical stability. One way is to measure the angle at which an object such as an empty film canister, with its center of gravity at its center near the cap end, tips over (see Figure 1.4). Place the canister on a flat surface, such as

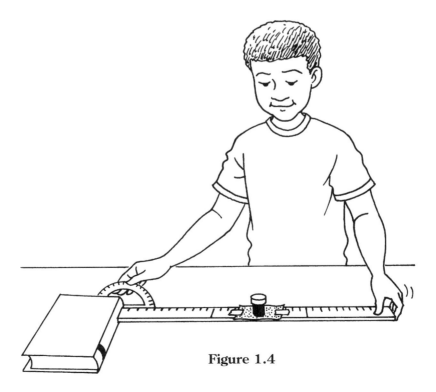

Figure 1.4

a yardstick (meterstick), and use a protractor to measure the angle of the measuring stick at which the canister tips over. Tape a piece of sandpaper on the surface to keep the canister from sliding. One edge of the yardstick (meterstick) should be placed against a heavy book so the yardstick does not slide as you lift the other edge.

b. The position of the center of gravity of the canister can be lowered by filling the canister one-fourth full with modeling clay. Repeat the experiment, pressing the clay against the bottom of the canister so the clay stays in place. The center of gravity of the canister is near its clay-filled bottom.

c. An object falls over when its center of gravity is not on an imaginary vertical line that passes through the base of the object. How does the width of the base affect mechanical stability? Using the previous investigation for testing stability, test objects with varied base sizes.

d. The center of gravity can be located outside the balancing object. For example, tightrope walkers are able to more easily balance when they hold a curved bar with weights on its ends that extend below the rope they walk on (see Figure 1.5 on page 15). The weight of the bar lowers the center of gravity of the tightrope walker to a point below the rope. Design a way to demonstrate this, such as by using a tightrope walker cut from a 4-inch (10-cm) –square piece of corrugated cardboard. *Note:* The cardboard grooves must run left and right, not up and down. Insert a 12-inch (30-cm) pipe cleaner through the bottom of the cardboard, and add metal washers to the ends to represent the weights on the pole. Balance the figure on a stretched string. Redesign the figure and/or move the pipe cleaner to determine the answers to the following questions:

- Is it easier for a tall or a short tightrope walker to balance on the wire?

- Which helps more—a short or a long balancing pole?

- Does the distance the pole is held above the wire affect the stability of the figure? The center of gravity of the figure is on an imaginary line running through the balancing point, and is below the body of the cardboard figure.

Get the Facts

The *center of mass* is the point on an object where the whole mass of the object appears to be concentrated. On Earth, the center of mass and the center of gravity of an object are at the same place. However, for larger

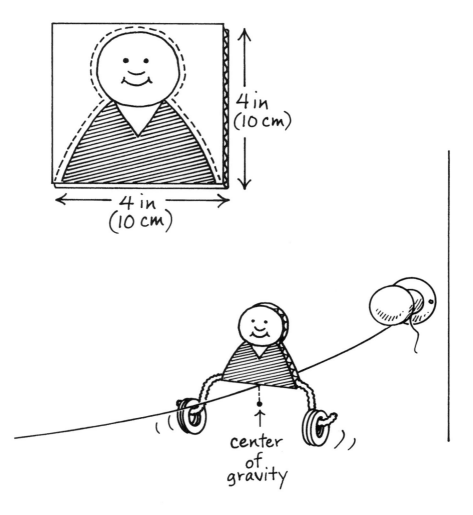

4 in
(10 cm)

4 in
(10 cm)

center
of
gravity

Figure 1.5

objects, such as planets and moons, the location of the center of mass will be slightly different from that of the center of gravity. How does the size of the object affect the location of the center of gravity? For information, see P. Erik Gundersen, *The Handy Physics Answer Book* (Detroit: Visible Ink, 1999), p. 106.

Mechanical Stability: Resistance to Falling Over

2

Some toys are designed so that when they are pushed, they may wobble back and forth but they don't fall down. No matter how far this kind of toy is pushed, it returns to its upright position. This ability to be moved and to return to the original position is an example of mechanical stability. An object is in equilibrium when all the forces acting on it are balanced. There are three types of equilibrium—stable, unstable, and neutral.

In this project, you will move different objects and trace the paths of their centers of gravity. You will investigate the effect of the height of an object's center of gravity, as well as the width of the object's base, on mechanical stability. You will construct an object with great mechanical stability, or stable equilibrium. You will also learn about the differences among stable, unstable, and neutral equilibriums.

Getting Started

Purpose: To model the motion of an object's center of gravity when the object is tilted.

Materials
pencil
ruler
6-by-10-inch (15-by-25-cm) piece of poster board
2-by-8-inch (5-by-20-cm) piece of poster board
one-hole paper punch
4-by-8-inch (5-by-20-cm) piece of graph paper
transparent tape

Procedure
1. Use the pencil and ruler to draw a line across the large piece of poster board, 2 inches (5 cm) from one long edge. This will be line A.

2. Draw a line down the center of the small strip of poster board from one short edge to the other. Make a dot in the center of this line. Using the paper punch, make a hole through the poster board at this dot.

3. Label one short edge of the poster board strip "Bottom," then cut a second hole in the strip in the right corner of the bottom edge.

4. Lay the small strip of poster board on the larger piece of poster board so that their bottom edges are together and the left side of the strip is on line A.

5. Use the pencil to trace the bottom hole in the strip on the large piece of poster board. Lift the paper strip and use the paper hole-punch to cut out the tracing on the poster board.

6. Lay the strip on the large piece of poster board as in step 4. Then insert the paper brad through the holes (bottom hole in the strip and hole in the poster board). The brad will secure the two pieces together.

7. Lay the piece of graph paper under the paper strip and secure it with tape, then tape the large poster board piece to a table (see Figure 2.1).

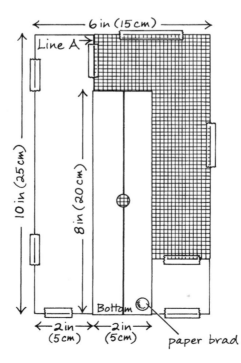

Figure 2.1

8. Hold the pencil with its point through the hole in the center of the poster board strip.

9. Use the pencil to rotate the poster board strip, marking a line to the edge of the graph paper.

10. Remove the pencil, then rotate the strip to the left and observe the path marked on the graph paper.

Results

The path on the graph paper shows that the hole in the poster board strip initially rises as the strip is rotated.

Why?

Since the poster board strip is symmetrical with uniform density, its center of gravity is in the center, where you made the hole. Before being rotated, the strip represents an object in **static equilibrium** (the state of an object that is not in motion, that is at rest). When rotated a small angular distance, the center of gravity of the poster board initially rises as indicated by the path of the hole traced on the paper. This demonstrates that if an object's center of gravity is in the center of the object, the center of gravity initially rises when the object is rotated or tilted slightly.

Try New Approaches

What effect does the location of the center of gravity have on an object's motion when that object is tilted? Cut two additional holes in the poster board strip, one 3 inches (7.5 cm) above the center hole and one 3 inches (7.5 cm) below the center hole. Repeat the experiment twice: First place the pencil in the top hole. This represents the higher center of gravity. Then repeat, placing the pencil in the bottom hole. This position represents a lower center of gravity. Compare the path of the center of gravity from the original experiment to the paths of the higher and lower centers of gravity.

Design Your Own Experiment

1. A ball has **neutral equilibrium,** the state of the object when pushing it over will not change the height of its center of gravity. Design a way to trace out the path of the center of gravity of a ball. One way is to cut a circle from corrugated cardboard, then make a hole in the center of the circle. (The circle represents a slice through the center of the ball, with the hole marking its center of gravity.) Place a sheet of paper on a table. Lay a book with a flat binding edge on the paper. Then lay the paper circle on the paper next to the binding edge of the book. Stand a pencil in the hole of the circle. Use the pencil to trace the motion of the hole as the circle is rolled across the edge of the book.

2. An object is in a state of **stable equilibrium** or **mechanical stability** when it falls back to its original position after being tilted slightly. This happens when the center of gravity of the object is initially raised during the object's rotation. Design an experiment to determine the effect of the height of the center of gravity on mechanical stability. One way is to fill two identical bottles with different amounts of water and seal the bottles. Fill one bottle about one-fourth full and the other totally full. (The more water, the higher the center of gravity.) Place the bottles side by side; tilt each bottle slightly, then release. Continue increasing the amount of the tilt until one of the bottles falls over. The first to fall will be the one with the lesser mechanical stability.

3. You can make a model that demonstrates mechanical stability (stable equilibrium) using a plastic egg. Find the kind of plastic egg that you can open. Shape a ball from a grape-size piece of clay. Open the egg and press the clay into the bottom of the more rounded end. Close the egg and stand it on that end. If the egg does not stand upright, reposition the clay. Give the standing egg a gentle push to one side. It should rock back and forth several times and stand upright again. If it lays on its side, remove some of the clay. For more information about the three types of equilibrium, see Mary Jones, *Physics* (New York: Cambridge University Press, 1997), pp. 50–51.

4. An object has stable equilibrium as long as a vertical arrow from the center of gravity of an object passes through its base (side it rests on) (see Figure 2.2). Design a way to determine how the width of the base affects the mechanical stability of an object. One way is to use a block of wood with edges of different

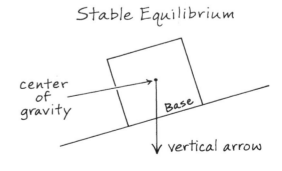

Figure 2.2

lengths, such as a 2-by-4-by-6-inch (5-by-10-by-15-cm) block. Let the base of the block be one of the 2-by-6-inch sides. Set the block near one end of a shallow baking pan or piece of stiff cardboard. To prevent the block from sliding, place a length of clay on the pan in front of the block. The width of the base is determined by measuring the side adjacent to the clay, as shown in Figure 2.3. Slowly raise the end of the pan opposite the clay until the block falls over. Hold the board in this position and ask a helper to measure the angle the board is raised above the table. Repeat three or more times, and average the measured angles. Rotate the block so that one of the 2-inch (5-cm) edges of the base faces the clay. Then repeat as before, determining

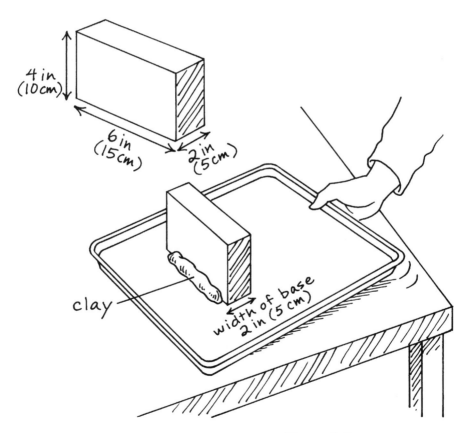

Figure 2.3

the average angle that the board must be raised for the block to fall. Use the results to explain how the width of the base of an object being tilted affects the angle at which the object will tip over.

Get the Facts

Objects that are in motion but are not accelerating are in equilibrium. What is the difference between linear and rotational equilibrium? How do static and dynamic equilibrium compare? For information, see Corinne Stockley, *Illustrated Dictionary of Physics* (London: Usborne, 2000), p. 15.

3 Friction: Force That Resists Motion

Friction is a force that resists motion and occurs whenever anything moves while in contact with anything else. Everyday actions such as sweeping, brushing your teeth, and turning a doorknob all involve friction. Without friction you couldn't hold on to the broom, toothbrush, or doorknob. Your hand would slip and slide the way your shoes do on ice. Friction also results in the slowing of moving objects. A thrown baseball or Frisbee rubs against air as it moves, and the friction of this contact slows its motion.

In this project, you will measure the static friction (force needed to move an object) of an object. You will discover the difference between an object's static friction and sliding friction (force needed to keep an object moving at a uniform speed). And you will discover which of these types of friction is greater. You will also calculate different types of coefficient of friction (ratio between the force of friction and the weight of the object being moved).

Getting Started

Purpose: To measure the static friction of an object.

Materials

6-by-12-inch (15-by-30-cm) piece of cardboard
transparent tape
9-ounce (270-ml) plastic cup
16-inch (40-cm) piece of string
rubber band (a #1, medium-size, band works well)
scissors
metric graph paper with 1-cm squares
20 marbles
pencil

Procedure

1. Place the cardboard on a table.
2. Tape the cup to the center of one of the shorter sides of the cardboard near the edge.
3. Tie the string around the bottom of the cup. Then tie one of the free ends of the string to the rubber band. You want the rubber band to be as close to the cup as possible. Cut off the excess ends of the string.
4. Lay the graph paper on the cardboard, with one edge next to the cup. Secure the paper to the cardboard with tape.
5. Add the marbles to the cup.
6. With the point of the pencil inside the loop of the rubber band, pull the rubber band straight but do not stretch it.
7. With the rubber band in this position, make a mark on the graph paper. Then move the pencil in a straight path away from the cup, stretching the rubber band and tracing a line on the graph paper with the pencil point (see Figure 3.1).
8. Stop moving the pencil as soon as the cardboard moves forward.

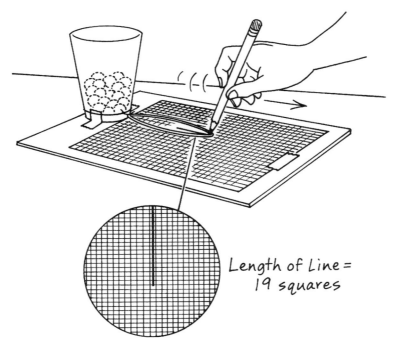

Length of Line = 19 squares

Figure 3.1

9. Count the squares that your pencil crossed. For partial squares, estimate the fractions. Record the number of squares in a Friction Data table like Table 3.1.

10. Repeat steps 7 through 9 four times. Average the results of all five tests, and record the average in the Friction Data table.

Table 3.1 Friction Data						
Surface/ Marbles in Cup	**Squares**					
	Trial 1	Trial 2	Trial 3	Trial 4	Trial 5	Average
table/20						

Results

You will be able to stretch the rubber band some distance before the cardboard moves. The exact results will depend on the elasticity of the rubber band as well as the surface of the table and the weight of the cup.

Why?

Friction is the name of forces that oppose the motion of one surface relative to another when the two surfaces are in contact with each other. Friction acts parallel to the surfaces in contact and in the opposite direction of motion. Friction is due to the fact that no matter how smooth the **macroscopic** (large enough to be seen with the naked eye) view of a surface, its **microscopic** (so small it requires a microscope to be seen) view is rough. The irregularities on both surfaces that are rubbing against each other interlock and offer resistance to motion. **Static friction** is the force that opposes the start of motion of an object.

In this investigation, the distance the rubber band stretches (length of line in number of squares) indicates the force of static friction between the surface of the cardboard and the surface of the table. The more the rubber band stretches before the cardboard moves, indicated by the number of squares crossed by the line, the greater the force of static friction.

Try New Approaches

1. How does the smoothness of the surfaces affect static friction? Repeat the investigation, placing the cardboard on different surfaces, such as waxed paper and different grades of sandpaper, that have been secured to the table.

2. How does the force pressing the surfaces together affect static friction? Repeat the original investigation, increasing the weight on the cardboard by adding more marbles to the cup.

3. How does lubrication affect static friction? Repeat the investigation twice: First use a surface of sandpaper alone. Then use sandpaper covered with a thick layer of petroleum jelly.

Design Your Own Experiment

1a. Design a way to measure the static friction of a system. One way is to attach one end of a string to a small box and the other end to a paper cup. Set another cup filled with marbles in the box, and place the box on a table so that the empty paper cup hangs over the edge of the table. The box should start out about 6 inches (15 cm) from the edge of the table. Add weights to the empty hanging cup until the box system (box and contents) starts to move. This weight equals the static friction (F_f) of the system. For weights, use some-

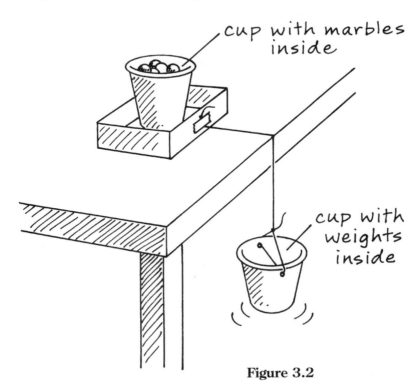

cup with marbles inside

cup with weights inside

Figure 3.2

thing like coins, paper clips, and/or washers that you know the individual weight of. Ask your teacher or a pharmacist to weigh whichever materials you choose on an accurate scale.

b. Friction between any two surfaces can be measured by the **coefficient of static friction,** which is the ratio between the force of static friction between two surfaces in contact with each other and the force holding the surfaces together. The coefficient of static friction is a constant that depends on the nature of the surfaces in contact with each other. Determine the coefficient of static friction between the cardboard and the material on the table's surface using this equation:

$$\mu = F_f / F_N$$

In this equation, μ (mu) is the symbol for the coefficient of static friction when F_f is the static friction (the total weight in the hanging cup) when the box moves, and F_N is the perpendicular force pushing the surfaces together (on a horizontal surface, the weight of the box and its contents). For information about the coefficient of static friction for common surfaces, see a physics text.

2a. **Sliding friction** is the frictional force between objects that are sliding with respect to one another. Using the materials from the previous investigation, start by removing about half of the weights from the hanging cup. Then slowly add the weights to the hanging cup one at a time, but this time after each addition, give the box a slight push toward the edge of the table where the cup is hanging. Continue this process until the box starts to move at a uniform **velocity** (speed and direction of a moving object). (If the box **accelerates**—changes in velocity per time—the force is too large; if the box stops, the force is too small.) How does the sliding friction compare to the static friction of the box?

b. How does the contact area of surfaces affect sliding friction? Design a way to measure the sliding friction of a system in which only the surface area changes. One way is to replace the box with a block of wood with different-size faces. Then determine the sliding friction of the wood for each of its different-size faces.

c. Determine the **coefficient of sliding friction** (the ratio between the force of sliding friction between surfaces in contact with each other and the force holding the surfaces together) for the box and table surfaces using the equation $\mu = F_f / F_N$, where μ (mu) is the symbol for sliding friction when F_f is the sliding friction.

Get the Facts

1. You can move one object across another without sliding, and thus without sliding friction, using rollers. What are ball bearings and, when placed between surfaces, how do ball bearings minimize sliding friction? For information, see Louis A. Bloomfield, *How Things Work: The Physics of Everyday Life* (New York: Wiley, 1997), pp. 57–60.

2. Brakes on a car work because of friction. Why are brakes generally designed to be applied to the front wheels before the rear wheels? For an exploratory investigation to discover the answer to this question, see Robert Gardner, *Experiments with Motion* (Springfield, N.J.: Enslow Publishers, 1995), pp. 63–67.

Surface Tension: A Liquid's Skinlike Property

4

The shapes of raindrops and soap bubbles are caused by cohesion (attractive force between like molecules) between molecules on the surface of the liquid. At the surface of any liquid, the molecules attract each other. Consequently, the surface layer is in tension, called surface tension, which causes the surface of the liquid to act like an elastic skin containing the liquid.

In this project, you will study surface tension and the effect that surfactants (materials that reduce the surface tension of liquids) have on it. You will determine the effect that changes in surface tension can have on the motion of a liquid. You will also explore how surface tension affects the shapes of drops of water and other liquids. And you will investigate the best soap-and-water combination for blowing the largest bubbles.

Getting Started

Purpose: To study surface tension.

Materials
cereal bowl
tap water
scissors
paper towel
small paper clip
toothpick

Procedure
1. Fill the bowl about three-fourths full with water.

2. Cut a piece about 2 inches (5 cm) square from the paper towel.

3. Place the paper clip in the center of the paper square.

4. Supporting the paper square by its edges, place the paper on the surface of the water in the bowl. The paper should float on the water with the paper clip on top of the paper.

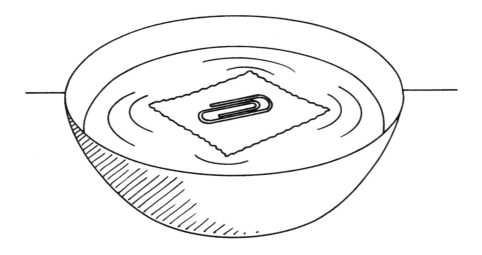

Figure 4.1

5. Using the toothpick, carefully push the paper down so that it sinks, leaving the paper clip on the water's surface.

6. Observe the floating paper clip and determine if any part is above and if any part is below the water's surface.

Results

The paper clip is resting on the surface of the water. No part of the clip is below the water's surface. The water is depressed slightly around the clip.

Why?

Surface tension is the **cohesion** (attractive force between like molecules) between molecules in the plane of the surface of a liquid. This **tension** (stretching force) causes the surface of the liquid to act like an elastic, skinlike covering. Beneath the surface of water, each molecule of water is attracted equally in all directions by neighboring water molecules. These molecules cannot move closer together because they are surrounded on all sides. At the surface, however, the top layer of water molecules is attracted to other water molecules to the sides and downward, but not upward. This results in a net downward force, causing the top layer of water to be slightly compressed. This compressed layer acts like a tightly stretched skin or film, which is strong enough to support lightweight objects, such as the paper clip in this investigation. Things **float** (state of being suspended in or resting on the surface of a **fluid**— any liquid or gaseous material that can flow) when placed in water if their density is equal to or less than that of water. But the paper clip's density is greater than that of water; thus it floats because the water's surface tension supports it. This is indicated by the fact that none of the paper clip is below the water's surface. Instead, the weight of the paper clip stretches the surface of the water downward, as you can see by the depression of the water around the paper clip. For more information about floating, see Chapter 12, "Buoyancy: Upward Force by Fluids."

Try New Approaches

Detergent is called a surface-active agent, or a **surfactant,** because it accumulates at a liquid's surface and reduces the surface tension of the liquid. What effect would a surfactant have on the results of the experiment? Repeat the experiment using water in which ½ teaspoon (2.5 ml) of liquid dishwashing detergent has been dissolved.

Design Your Own Experiment

1. A drop of surfactant in water immediately weakens the surface tension where the surfactant enters the water. Design a way to show how differences in surface tension can cause a liquid to flow. One way is to add just enough water to cover the bottom of a plate. Let the plate stand for about 1 minute to allow motion of the water to stop. Place one drop of food coloring on the edge of the water. Wet one end of a toothpick with liquid detergent and touch this wet end to the colored spot in the water. Observe any motion of the colored water.

2. Surfactants weaken surface tension. How does the concentration of a surfactant affect surface tension? Design a way to determine how the concentration of a surfactant affects surface tension. One way is to cover the bottom of a small plate with water. Place two round toothpicks on the surface of the water. With a third toothpick, move

the floating sticks so they are close together. Wet the end of the toothpick you're holding with liquid detergent and then touch the wet end to the water between the two floating toothpicks (see Figure 4.2). Observe the speed at which the two toothpicks move. The greater the speed, the greater the substance's effectiveness at lowering the water's surface tension. Repeat the investigation four times, using clean water, new toothpicks, and different concentrations of detergent. The detergent concentrations can be made using the combinations in Table 4.1. The materials can be measured with an eyedropper, combined on a sheet of waxed paper, and each stirred with a separate toothpick.

Table 4.1 Detergent Concentration		
Detergent Concentration, Percent	Water, Drops	Liquid Detergent, Drops
100	0	1
75	1	3
50	1	1
25	3	1
0	1	0

Rate the effect of the different concentrations on their ability to lower surface tension using a distance scale from 0 to 5 to compare the distances the toothpicks move, with 0 being the least distance. Record the distance rating for each detergent concentration in a Surface Tension Data table like Table 4.2.

Table 4.2 Surface Tension Data	
Detergent Concentration, Percent	Distance Rating, 0 to 5
100	
75	
50	
25	
0	

Figure 4.2

Use this information to prepare a graph comparing detergent concentration with its effect on lowering surface tension. For more information about the effect of concentration of surfactants on surface tension, see Carl H. Snyder, *The Extraordinary Chemistry of Ordinary Things* (New York: Wiley, 1998), pp. 322–330.

3. Surface tension is also the reason why unconfined liquids form drops. The net inward force on the surface molecules of water causes the surface to become as small as possible. A sphere is the shape that has the least surface for a given volume. Design a way to show the shapes of drops of liquids that have weak surface tension. One way is to use different concentrations of a detergent solution (as listed in Table 4.1). Use an eyedropper to place 1 drop of each solution onto waxed paper, and compare the roundness of each drop. Rate the roundness of each drop on a scale of 0 to 5, with 0 being the least round.

4. Detergents reduce the surface tension of water, which makes the surface of water stretchier. This is why bubbles can be made with soapy water. Determine the best soap-and-water combination for blowing the largest bubbles. Does glycerin (found in most pharmacies) have an effect on the surface tension of water? Try using glycerin in your bubble solution to see what effect it might have.

Get the Facts

1. Water molecules have hydrogen bonds. How do these bonds affect surface tension? For information, see a chemistry text.

2. Water is not always wet. What can this mean? What does the wetness of water depend on? How can the wetness of water be increased? For information about making water wet, see Robert L. Wolke, *What Einstein Didn't Know* (New York: Dell, 1997), pp. 194–195.

5 | Work: Force through a Distance

"Work" is a term used in physics to indicate that a force has caused an object to move. A tennis player hitting a tennis ball with a racket is an example of work because the tennis ball moves when struck by the racket. But work is not done every time a force is applied. For example, if you push against a building for several minutes, you may become tired, but no work has been done. This is because the building did not move. The amount of work done is determined by multiplying the force applied to an object by the distance the object moves in the direction of the force. The SI (internationally agreed-upon method of using the metric system of measurement) unit for work is joule if the SI units for force and distance, respectively, are newton and meter.

In this project, you will learn how to measure the work done on an object. You will determine the effect that a simple machine has on work. You will also determine the effect of the direction of the force on work.

Getting Started

Purpose: To measure the work done on an object.

Materials
brick (or any object of comparable weight)
shoe box large enough to hold the brick
paper hole-punch
5-pound (2200-g) spring scale with a hook
yardstick (meterstick)
masking tape

Procedure
1. Place the brick inside the box.

2. Use the paper hole-punch to cut a hole in the end of the box. Attach the scale's hook through the hole in the box (see Figure 5.1).

3. Place the box at one end of a table. Place a piece of masking tape 6 inches (15 cm) in front of the box. This will be the starting line.

4. Measure the distance from the starting line to the end of the table toward which you are pulling in **meters (m)**—an SI unit for distance. Record this as distance traveled *(d)* in a Work Data table, like Table 5.1.

5. Pull the scale so that the scale and box move horizontally across the table at a constant speed. Determine the scale reading when the box crosses the start line. This force must be measured in **newtons (N)**—an SI unit for force. Record the newton force in the Work Data table. If your scale measures in pounds, convert pounds to newtons using this conversion: 1 pound = 4.45 N. For example, if the measurement is 2 pounds, the newton force would be 2 pounds × 4.45 N /1 pound = 8.9 N. If the scale measures in grams, convert grams to newtons using this conversion: 1 g = 0.0098 N. For example, if the measurement is 908 g, the newton force would be 908 g × 0.0098 N/1g = 8.9 N.

6. Repeat step 5 four times and average the measurements.

7. Calculate the work done on the box using this equation: $w = f \times d$.

In the equation, w equals work, f is the force acting on the box in newtons, and d is the distance (in meters) the box moves during the time the force is being measured. For example, if f = 8.9 N and d = 0.5 m, then w = 8.9 N × 0.5 m = 4.45 Nm.

Note: 1 Nm = 1 joule (J). **Joule (J)** is an SI unit for work.

So for this example the work done is 4.45 J.

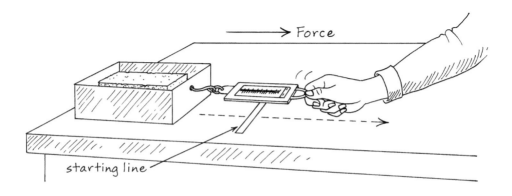

Figure 5.1

Table 5.1 Work Data							
Distance (d), m	Force (f), N						Work (w), J
	Trial 1	Trial 2	Trial 3	Trial 4	Trial 5	Average	$w = f \times d$

Results

The work done will depend on the force needed to pull the box and the distance it moves. In the example, the work done is 4.45 J.

Why?

Work is what is accomplished when a force causes an object to move. The amount of work done is equal to the product of the force applied to an object times the distance the object moves in the direction of the force. Another requirement for work to be done is that the distance the object is moved must be in the same direction that the force is applied. In this experiment, a horizontal force moves the box in a horizontal direction, so work is done.

Try New Approaches

1. Does the speed at which an object moves affect the work needed to move it? Repeat the experiment twice, first at a higher but constant speed and then at a lower but constant speed.

2. How does the weight of the object being moved affect the work done to move it? Repeat the original experiment twice, first using a lesser weight in the box and then using a greater weight. *Note:* Try to pull the box at the same speed for each testing.

Design Your Own Experiment

1. A **machine** is a device that makes work easier. Machines make work easier by changing either the size or the direction of the input force. **Simple machines** are the most basic machines, such as an **inclined plane** (a flat, slanted surface). Inclined planes are used to transport an object to a specific height. Design an experiment to determine if using an inclined plane affects the overall work done on the object being moved. One way is to add weight, such as marbles, clay, or coins, to a small box with a lid. Close the box and secure the lid with tape. Tie a string around the box and attach the hook of a

spring scale to the string. Use the scale to slowly raise the box a vertical distance of 1 meter. As you raise the box, ask a helper to note the reading on the scale in newtons, grams, or pounds. If the reading moves up and down slightly, record the average reading. Employ the previous method of determining force in newtons using pound or gram units. Then determine the work done in lifting the box using this equation: $w = f \times d$. Then prepare an inclined plane by placing one end of a board at least 1 meter longer than the box on a stack of several books. Use the scale to move the box up the inclined plane for a distance of 1 meter. Repeat the procedure for determining the force needed to move the box and the work done. Use diagrams to display the results of the experiments.

2a. Sometimes a force on an object is at an angle to the direction of motion. An example would be pulling a wagon's handle at an angle, causing the wagon to move horizontally (see Figure 5.2). In this case, the relationship of the force acting on the wagon can be expressed by the equation $d_a/d_h = f_h/f_a$, where d_a is the distance of the side adjacent to the angle of the applied force, d_h is the distance of the hypotenuse (side opposite the right angle), f_h is the force causing horizontal motion parallel to the direction in which an object is moved, and f_a is the force applied at angle A°. The **cosine (cos)** of an angle is equal to the length of the adjacent side (d_a) divided by the hypotenuse (d_b). Since $\cos A° = d_a/d_h$ and $d_a/d_h = f_h/f_a$, then $\cos A° = f_h/f_a$. Thus the horizontal force (f_h) causing the wagon to move in a horizontal direction can be calculated using this equation: $f_h = f_a \times \cos A°$. (See Appendix 1 for the cosine value of different angles.)

Design an experiment to calculate the work done by a force that is at an angle to the direction in which an object is moved. One way is to attach a scale to a weighted box. Move the box across a table by pulling on the scale so that this force is at an angle to the movement of the box, as shown in Figure 5.3. Measure and record the distance *(d)* the box is moved. Use a protractor to measure the angle (A°) of the applied force. Determine the work using this equation:

$$w = (f_a \cos A°) \times d$$

For example, if the box is moved 0.6 m by a force of 10 N applied at an angle of 30°, the work done would be:

$$w = (10\,\text{N} \times \cos 30°) \times 0.6\,\text{m}$$
$$= 10\,\text{N} \times 0.87 \times 0.6\text{m}$$
$$= 5.22\,\text{Nm or } 5.22\,\text{J}$$

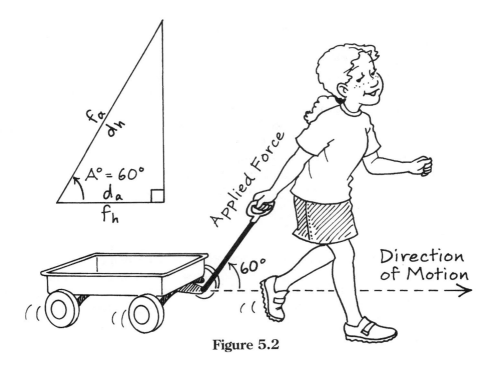

Figure 5.2

For more information about work done by a constant force that is applied at an angle relative to the direction of motion, see J. P. Den Martog, *Mechanics* (New York: Dover, 1961), pp. 133–135.

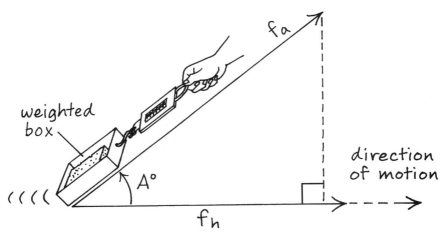

Figure 5.3

b. How does the angle affect the amount of work done in the previous experiment? Repeat the experiment three times, first at a smaller angle and second at a greater angle, but less than 90°. For the third trial, use an angle of 90°, thus slightly lifting the box above the table. Prove mathematically that while the box is moved horizontally while applying a force at 90°, no work is done. **Science Fair Hint:** Show vector diagrams for each angle. You do work in lifting an object, but once the object is lifted, you do no work in carrying it across a room. For an explanation of this seeming paradox, see *work* in a physics text and Larry Gonick and Art Hufamn, *The Cartoon Guide to Physics* (New York: HarperPerennial, 1990), p. 75.

Get the Facts

Power is the rate of doing work. Since power is work divided by time, power is expressed as joules per second in SI units. The power unit of watt was named after James Watt (1736–1819), the inventor of the steam engine. How do the units of watt and horsepower compare to the SI unit of joules/sec? See a physics text for a comparison of power units.

Newton's Third Law of Motion: Action-Reaction

Sir Isaac Newton (1642–1727), the famous British scientist credited with discovering gravity, also gave us three laws describing motion. Newton's first law of motion states that a force is needed to change the motion of an object. In other words, a force either starts an object moving or causes a moving object to stop. His second law of motion explains how the force needed to accelerate (change in velocity) an object depends on the mass of the object. His third law explains that forces act in pairs.

In this project, you will demonstrate Newton's third law of motion, that every action has an equal and opposite reaction due to the action of forces in pairs. You will also determine how pairs of forces that are equal but in opposite directions can produce motion.

Getting Started

Purpose: To demonstrate Newton's third law of motion.

Materials
pencil
5-ounce (150-ml) paper cup
40 to 50 pennies
12-inch (30-cm) piece of string
handheld spring scale

Procedure
1. Use the pencil to make two holes across from each other just beneath the rim of the cup. Place the coins in the cup.
2. Loop the string through the holes, then tie the ends of the string between the holes.
3. Hold the scale and adjust it so that it reads zero.

4. While holding the scale, attach the cup so that the cup hangs freely. Observe the reading on the scale.

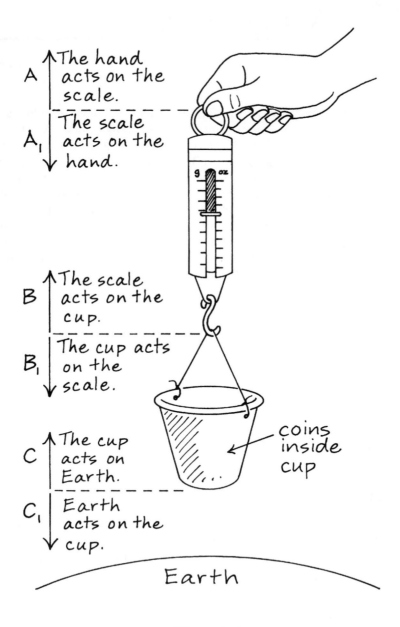

Figure 6.1

Results

The cup pulls the scale down so that the measurement on the scale indicates the weight of the cup and the coins.

Why?

Newton's third law of motion states that for every action, there is an equal and opposite reaction due to pairs of forces. In other words, Newton realized that if one object applies a force on another, the second object applies an equal force but in the opposite direction on the first object. You can be sure that two forces are action-reaction pairs of forces if the reverse description of one force describes the other force. In Figure 6.1, the three identified action-reaction pairs of forces are: A/A_1; B/B_1; C/C_1. The description of force A is "the hand acts on the scale," and the description of force A_1 is "the scale acts on the hand." One description is the reverse of the other, so the forces are equal in magnitude, but in opposite directions. Thus forces A and A_1 are action-reaction pairs.

Try New Approaches

The scale attached to the cup measures the downward force of the cup (the action). How can the upward force of the hand (the reaction) be measured? Repeat the experiment, using two scales. First hang one scale from the other. So that the weights of the scales are not considered, while holding the top scale (A), adjust the scales so each reads zero. Attach the cup to the bottom scale (B) as before. Scale A measures the upward force (the reaction), and scale B measures the downward force (the action).

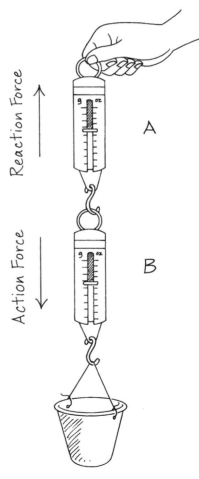

Figure 6.2

Science Fair Hint: A diagram showing the action-reaction pairs can be used as part of a project display.

Design Your Own Experiment

1. Every force on an object causes the object to be compressed to some degree. Design an experiment to demonstrate that an object compresses until the action-reaction forces are equal. For example, fill a 3-ounce (90-ml) cup with coins. Lay two similar-size books about 10 inches (25 cm) apart on a table. Support the ends of a thin, flexible, plastic ruler on the books. Set the cup of coins in the center of the ruler.

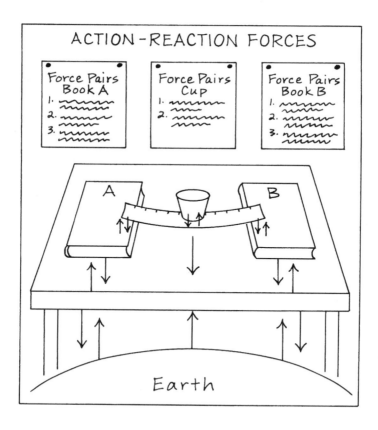

Figure 6.3

Science Fair Hint: Make a diagram showing the compression of the ruler and the action-reaction pairs of forces, such as in Figure 6.3. Three legends describing the force pairs of the books and the cup can be added to the drawing. For example:

Force Pairs, Book A

- Ruler acts on book A.
  Book A acts on ruler.
- Book A acts on table.
  Table acts on book A.
- Table acts on Earth.
  Earth acts on table.

2. Unaccompanied forces do not exist. Since all forces are in pairs of equal strength and acting in opposite directions and acting on different objects, what causes motion? A **resultant force** is the single force that has the same effect as the sum of two or more forces acting simultaneously on an object. When forces simultaneously act on an object and the resultant force is zero, the forces are said to be **balanced forces** and produce no acceleration. **Acceleration** is a change in **velocity** (speed and direction of a moving object) per unit of time. When the resultant force of a group of forces acting simultaneously on an object is not equal to zero, the forces are said to be **unbalanced forces.** Newton's first law of motion explains that an unbalanced force acting on the object is needed to cause acceleration. In this law, the resultant force is the **net force** (the sum of all forces acting simultaneously on an object).

   Design an experiment to demonstrate that a pair of action-reaction forces are unbalanced because they act on different objects. One way is with two identical balloons. Inflate one of the balloons and tie a knot in its open end. Lay the balloon on a table and observe any motion of the balloon. Repeat using an inflated balloon that is not tied.

   Science Fair Hint: Prepare a diagram representing the action-reaction forces for the open and closed balloon, such as in Figure 6.4. Add the calculations for determining the net force of the gas inside the balloon on the balloon, represented by forces A as well as the net force of the balloon on the gas inside the balloon, represented by forces B. The equation for net force is:

$$f_{(\text{net force})} = (f\uparrow + f\downarrow) + (f\rightarrow + f\leftarrow)$$

The calculation for determining the net force of the gas on the balloon in the closed balloon is:

$$f_{(net\ force)} = (f\uparrow + f\downarrow) + (f\rightarrow + f\leftarrow)$$
$$= (A_1\uparrow + A_3\downarrow) + (A_2\rightarrow + A_4\leftarrow)$$
$$= 0 + 0$$
$$= 0$$

The equation representing the net forces of the gas acting on the open balloon is:

$$f_{(net\ force)} = (f\uparrow + f\downarrow) + (f\rightarrow + f\leftarrow)$$
$$= (A_1\uparrow) + (A_2\rightarrow + A_3\leftarrow)$$
$$= A_1\uparrow + 0$$
$$= A_1\uparrow$$

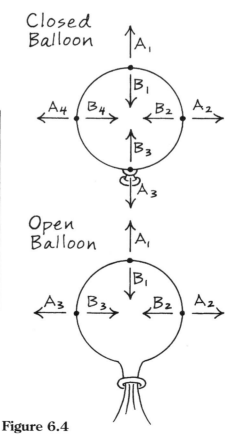

Legend	
Forces	Description
A	Gas inside balloon is acting on balloon.
B	Balloon is acting on gas inside balloon.

Figure 6.4

In the closed balloon, the action reaction pairs are A_1/B_1, A_2/B_2, A_3/B_3, and A_4/B_4. As shown by the calculations, the net force of the gas acting on the balloon is zero. Therefore there is no unbalanced force, and thus no motion of the balloon caused by the gas acting on it. In the open balloon, the action reaction pairs are also A_1/B_1, A_2/B_2, and A_3/B_3. As shown by the calculations, the net force of the gas acting on the balloon is equal to force $A_1\uparrow$. While $A_1\uparrow$ and $B_1\downarrow$ are action-reaction pairs acting in different directions, they each act on different objects, thus are unbalanced forces. The unbalanced force of $A_1\uparrow$ acting on the balloon, causes the balloon to move in the direction of this force. Use the net force equation to calculate the net force of the balloon on the gas inside the open and closed balloon to determine why the gas moves out of the open balloon.

Get the Facts

1. The use of steam as a source of power can be traced back to a toy invented by a Greek engineer named Hero of Alexandria (20?–62?). This toy turned as a result of action-reaction forces. For information about the construction of Hero's toy and how the action-reaction forces were produced, see Struan Reid and Patricia Fara, *Inventors* (Tulsa, Okla.: EDC, 1994), p. 10.

2. A Hero's engine can be made from a soda can. For information about building this simple Hero's engine and making predictions about its movement, see Robert Ehrlich, *Why Toast Lands Jelly-Side Down* (Princeton, N.J.: Princeton University Press, 1997), pp. 69–71.

Terminal Velocity: Maximum Velocity in a Fluid

7

The term "free fall" is commonly used to indicate the condition of an object falling toward Earth. Examples include a parachutist in the part of his or her jump before the parachute opens, or a falling ball. In physics, an object is said to be in free fall if the only force acting on the object is gravity. An object doesn't have to be falling "straight down" to be free-falling; the only requirement is that gravity is the only force acting on it. So when a ball is thrown up, even when it is rising, it is in free fall. Once it leaves your hand, if you neglect air resistance (the retarding force of air on objects moving through it), gravity is the only force acting on the ball.

In this project you will determine the effect of the shape and weight of a falling object on acceleration. You will calculate the terminal, or final, velocity of an object in free fall and compare it to the actual terminal (final) velocity of an object falling through Earth's atmosphere. You will also determine the effect of drag (the force of resistance on an object moving through a fluid) and weight on terminal velocity.

Getting Started

Purpose: To determine the effect of shape on the acceleration of falling objects.

Materials
2 basket-type coffee filters
ruler

Procedure
1. With your hands, slightly spread the sides of one of the coffee filters so that the diameter across its top is 1 to 2 inches (2.5 to 5 cm) greater than that of the other filter. Leave the sides of the other filter as vertical as possible.

2. With their open sides up, hold the filters, one in each hand, as high as possible and at the same height, then drop the filters at the same time. Determine which filter falls faster.

3. Repeat step 2 three or more times.

Results

The filter that is less spread out falls faster.

Figure 7.1

Why?

Velocity is the speed and direction of a moving object. Acceleration is a change in velocity per unit of time. **Free fall** is the motion of an object when the only force acting on it is gravity. In Earth's **gravitational field** (the region of space in which a force of gravity acts on objects), free fall takes place near Earth's surface at a constant acceleration of 32 ft/sec^2 (9.8 m/sec^2), and is known as **acceleration of free fall.** However, since Earth is surrounded by an **atmosphere** (blanket of gases surrounding a **celestial body**—natural objects in the sky, such as planets), falling objects collide with air molecules that exert an upward retarding force caused by the friction between the air and the surface of the object. (**Air** is the name for the mixture of gases in Earth's atmosphere.) This frictional force is called **drag** (the retarding force acting on an object moving through fluid, such as air or water). The greater the surface area of the falling object, the more air molecules the falling object strikes per second. An increase in the number of air molecules striking the surface of the falling object increases the upward force or drag on the object. With an increase in drag, the acceleration of the falling object decreases, as indicated by an increase in the time it takes the object to fall.

Try New Approaches

How does weight affect the acceleration of falling objects? Repeat the experiment using a single coffee filter and a double coffee filter, made by placing two coffee filters together, one within the other. The shapes of the coffee filters should be as similar as possible, so that weight is the only factor being tested. A difference in acceleration can be determined by the time of fall. The greater the time of fall, the lower the acceleration. Likewise, the slower the time of fall, the greater the acceleration.

Design Your Own Experiment

1. Design an experiment to determine the average falling time of an object at different heights. One way is to use a stopwatch to measure the time of descent of a coffee filter dropped from different heights. Tape a strip of paper to a wall, and starting at the floor, mark these heights on the paper strip: 0.5 m, 1.0 m, 1.5 m, and 2.0 m. Holding the coffee filter in line with but not touching the mark for 0.5 m, drop the filter and simultaneously start the stopwatch. Stop the watch when the filter hits the floor. Record the falling time in an Average Falling Time Data table like the one in Table 7.1. Repeat the

experiment at the 0.5 m height three or more times and average the times. Repeat the experiment at the remaining heights.

Table 7.1 Average Falling Time Data				
Distance, m	**Time, sec**			**Average Time, sec**
0.5				
1.0				
1.5				
2.0				

2a. Free-falling objects accelerate toward Earth at a rate of 9.8 m/sec². This means that if one neglects air friction, the velocity of a falling object increases in the direction of Earth 9.8 m/sec for every second it falls. The formula for calculating the time of a free-falling object is: $t = \sqrt{2d/g}$, which is read as time equals the square root of 2 times distance (height) divided by gravitational acceleration (9.8 m/sec²).

Use the formula to calculate the time of descent in the coffee filter free-falls from heights of 0.5 m, 1.0 m, 1.5 m, and 2.0 m. Record this time in a Calculated Falling Time Data table like the one in Table 7.2.

Table 7.2 Calculated Falling Time Data	
Distance, m	**Calculated Time, sec ($t = \sqrt{2d/g}$)**
0.5	
1.0	
1.5	
2.0	

b. When drag on a falling object due to air resistance equals the force weight of the falling object, the resultant force on the object equals zero, and the object stops accelerating. But the object does not stop moving—in fact, it continues to fall at a constant or final velocity, called **terminal velocity.** For each height, compare the average measured times of descent of the coffee filter in Table 7.1 with the calculated time of descent if the filter free falls. Determine the height at which the filter reaches terminal velocity. This can be expressed in reference to the height marks, such as before 0.5 m or between 0.5 m and 1.0 m. Note that once the filter reaches its terminal velocity, its falling time will increase because it is no longer accelerating. For more information about terminal velocity, see P. Erik Gundersen, *The Handy Physics Answer Book* (Detroit: Visible Ink, 1999), pp. 36–37.

3a. Design an experiment to determine how weight affects the terminal velocity of a falling object. One way is to use objects that are of different weights, but light enough to reach their terminal velocity quickly, such as a single coffee filter and a double or triple coffee filter. Keep the shape of the single and double coffee filters the same so their surface areas are the same. Tape a sheet of paper to a wall

Figure 7.2

and make a mark on it at 200 cm and 175 cm above the floor. Hold the single and double filters so they are in line with the 200-cm mark, then drop them. Ask a helper to note which reaches the floor first. Label this filter A; label the other filter B. Then hold filter A at a height of 200 cm and filter B at 175 cm. Release the filters to see if the lower height for filter B is enough to allow both filters to hit the floor at the same time. If not, continue lowering or raising filter B until both filters hit the floor simultaneously. Record the height of both filters.

b. The ratio of the heights at which filters A and B were released that resulted in their hitting the ground at the same time should be approximately equal to the ratio of their average velocities when dropped from this distance. This can be expressed as $h_A/h_B = v_A/v_B$.

Confirm this relationship by measuring the time it takes filter A to fall from 200 cm and for filter B to fall from the height determined in part 2a. Use the equation $v = d/t$, where d is the distance a filter falls (its height) and t is the time, to determine the average velocity of each. Compare this to the height ratios for the filters.

Get the Facts

1. Newton was the first to recognize that an unbalanced or net force causes something to accelerate. The relationship between force and acceleration is called *Newton's second law of motion*. What is the mathematical expression of Newton's second law? How can this expression be written if the force is the weight of an object and the acceleration is due to gravity? For information, see a physics textbook.

2. Because of the air around Earth, what is the maximum or terminal velocity of a sky diver? What is the terminal velocity once the parachute is open? For information see P. Erik Gundersen, *The Handy Physics Answer Book* (Detroit: Visible Ink, 1999), p. 38.

8 Linear Inertia: Resistance to Change in Linear Motion

Seat belts are put in cars to restrain people if the vehicles have to stop suddenly. A person in a car is going as fast as the car is, but when the car quickly decelerates (reduces its velocity in a given time), the person—who is not attached to the car—continues forward at the original velocity. This tendency of an object to continue in motion unless acted on by a force is called inertia. Inertia also describes the tendency of objects to continue to be stationary unless acted on by a force.

In this project, you will perform an investigation similar to one designed by Galileo Galilei (1564–1642) to determine the effect of net forces of varying amounts on the motion of an object. You also will design an inertia balance and use it to determine the mass (amount of matter) of objects.

Getting Started

Purpose: To show how a force affects the state of motion of an object.

Materials
pen
meterstick
4-by-28-inch (10-by-70-cm) piece of poster board
scissors
protractor
transparent tape
marble

Procedure
1. Construct a double-ramp using the following steps:
- Use the pen and measuring stick to draw two lines down the poster board 3 cm from each side.

54

- Mark each 1 cm down the center of the poster board strip.
- Fold up the edges of the strip at the lines you drew in step 1 to make outside rims.
- At the 15-cm and 25-cm marks, cut diagonal slits in the rim on both sides (see Figure 8.1).
- Bend the strip at each slit to form an incline of 60⁰ at each end of the strip. Use tape to secure the overlapped edges of the rims.

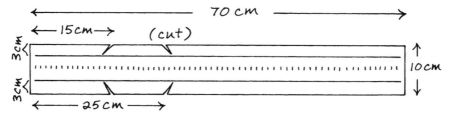

Figure 8.1

2. Set the double-ramp structure on a table. Use tape to secure the top of ramp A to a vertical structure, such as a wall. Tape the middle of the structure to the table. Ramp B should be stable enough to stand unsupported, but if necessary, use a book to support it.

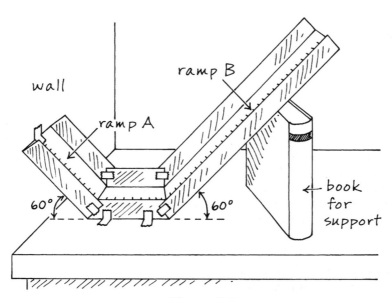

Figure 8.2

3. Hold the marble at the second centimeter mark from the top of ramp A (13 cm—from the base of ramp A).

4. Release the marble and allow it to roll down ramp A.

5. Observe the height the marble reaches on ramp B. Using the marks on the ramp, measure the distance the marble travels from the base of ramp B to this height. Record the measurement in a Distance Data table like Table 8.1.

6. Repeat steps 7 through 9 four times and average the results.

Table 8.1 Distance Data						
Initial height on ramp A (60°), cm	**Final height on ramp B (60°), cm**					
	Trial 1	Trial 2	Trial 3	Trial 4	Trial 5	Average
13	12	10	11	12	10	11

Results

The distance will vary depending on the size of the marble used and the surface of the ramp. The author's marble traveled an average 11 cm up ramp B.

Why?

The ramp structure you built is similar to the one designed by Galileo. Galileo discovered that when the surfaces of the **ramps** (inclined planes) are very smooth, a ball will roll down one ramp and rise to almost the same height on the opposite ramp. The author's ramp had more friction than did Galileo's structure, as indicated by the ball being released at 13 cm above the surface and rising an average of only 11 cm on the opposite ramp. Once the ball was released, the force of gravity pulled the ball down. When it reached the bottom of ramp A, the ball had reached its maximum velocity, v_{max}, and would have continued to move at this velocity if no forces acted on it. The tendency of an object to remain at rest or to resist any change in its state of motion unless acted on by an outside force is called **inertia.** In this investigation there were forces acting on the ball, including friction between the ball and the poster board ramp. As the ball rolled up the ramp, gravity pulled down on it, also causing **deceleration** (a decrease in velocity per unit of time). Deceleration is also called negative acceleration.

Try New Approaches

As the angle between ramp B and the surface decreases, the decelerating force on the ball decreases. How does the decrease in the decelerating force affect the distance the ball rolls up ramp B? Determine this by repeating the investigation three times, decreasing the angle of ramp B only to 40°, 20°, and 0°. Add an extension to ramp B if necessary. Using your results, explain how Galileo's results from a similar experiment made him aware that without an incline or friction, the ball would roll forever. In other words, how did Galileo determine that objects have inertia?

Design Your Own Experiment

1a. **Mass** is the amount of matter in an object and is a measure of inertia. As mass increases, inertia of an object increases. (**Matter** is the substance of which physical objects consist; anything that takes up space and has mass.) Design a way to determine the mass of an object by measuring its inertia. One way is to design and calibrate an **inertia balance,** which is an instrument that determines mass due to the **periodic motion** (the motion of an object, such as a back-and-forth motion, that is repeated in each of a succession of equal time intervals) of the balance. This can be done using a thin hacksaw blade and coins. To avoid being cut, cover the teeth of the blade with a strip of masking tape. Then tape the blade to the edge of a table. Fill an empty plastic 35-mm film canister about one-fourth full with modeling clay. Push the clay down so it is secure and its surface is relatively flat. Tape the canister to the free end of the blade. Push a cotton ball into the canister. Calibrate the balance (blade + canister) using a standard mass, such as a penny.

First determine the time of 25 oscillations with no pennies. Place the cap on the canister. Then cause the balance to **vibrate** (repeatedly swing or move back and forth) by pulling it to one side and releasing. Using a stopwatch, determine the time of 25 oscillations. Begin timing the oscillations as soon as you let go of the blade. One oscillation is when the film canister swings out then returns to its original position. Calculate the **period (T),** which is the time it takes a vibrating object to complete one **vibration** or **oscillation** (to swing or move back and forth) using this formula:

$$T = \text{period (time/oscillations)}$$

For example, if it takes 10 seconds for 25 oscillations, the period would be:

$$T = 10 \text{ sec}/25 \text{ oscillations}$$
$$= 0.4 \text{ sec/oscillation}$$

Record the period in an Inertia Data table like Table 8.2. Repeat the procedure four times and average the results. Then place one penny in the canister and repeat the procedure. Continue the procedure, adding one coin at a time until a total of 10 coins are used.

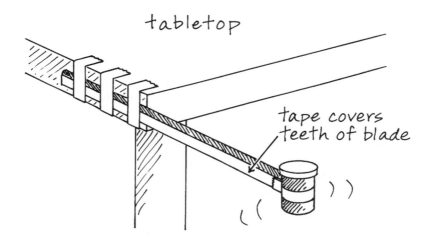

Figure 8.3

Table 8.2 Inertia Data						
Number of Coins, penny	**Period (T), sec**					
	Trial 1	Trial 2	Trial 3	Trial 4	Trial 5	Average
0						
1						
10						

b. Use a food scale to determine the mass in grams of one penny by measuring the mass of one hundred pennies and dividing by 100. Then use the mass of one penny to calculate the mass of each number of pennies from one to ten. Use the mass of each number of pennies and the period *(T)* for each number to create a mass vs. period graph with mass on the *x*-axis and period *(T)* on the *y*-axis.

c. The mass of an object, such as other coins or a metal washer that will fit in the canister, can be determined by measuring its time for 25 oscillations, calculating its period *(T)*, and comparing this period to mass on the mass vs. period graph from part b.

d. Another way to determine the mass of an object is to use the relationship between mass and period, which can be expressed by this equation:

$$m_1/m_2 = T_1^2/T_2^2$$

in which m_1 is the unknown mass and m_2 is the known mass (penny). T_1 and T_2 are their respective periods. To determine the unknown mass, the equation can be written as:

$$m_1 = m_2 \times T_1^2 \div T_2^2$$

Get the Facts

Galileo was one of many great scientists whom Sir Isaac Newton (1642—1727) said he was influenced by when he formed his ideas about motion. Newton described three laws of motion, the first being the law of inertia. How does inertia affect objects at rest? How does inertia affect the direction and the speed of an object in motion? For more information, see Robert Garner, *Experiments with Motion* (Springfield, N.J.: Enslow, 1995), pp. 7–17.

9 Rotational Motion: Spinning Objects

A rotating object spins about an axis, which is an imaginary line through the center of the object. This axis can be real, such as the axle of a wheel on a vehicle, or imaginary, such as that through a rolling ball or hoop. If an object is rolling down an incline or across a level plane, it is spinning about the axis as the axis is being translated (moved from one location to another). Mechanical energy is the energy of an object that is moving or has the potential of moving. For rotating objects, part of the mechanical energy is due to rotational energy.

In this project, you will compare the mechanical energy of rotating objects of different shapes—including different-size spheres, a hollow and a solid sphere, a cylinder, and hoops—on an incline and on a level surface.

Getting Started

Purpose To determine the effect of size on mechanical energy of two rotating spheres on an inclined plane.

Materials

2 or 3 books
12-by-36-inch (30-cm-by-90-cm) stiff cardboard
 (Size is not critical; a board of comparable size can be used.)
bath towel
marker
ruler
2 glass marbles of different radii

Procedure

1. Stack the books on the floor and make a ramp (an inclined plane) by supporting one short end of the cardboard on the pile of books.

2. Stretch the towel on the floor at the end of the cardboard ramp. This will help stop the spheres when they leave the ramp.

3. Use the marker to draw a line across the ramp about 4 inches (10 cm) from the top edge. Hold the edge of the ruler on this line, and place the marbles behind the ruler.

4. Lift the ruler to allow the marbles to roll down the ramp. Observe the marbles and determine which one reaches the end of the ramp first.

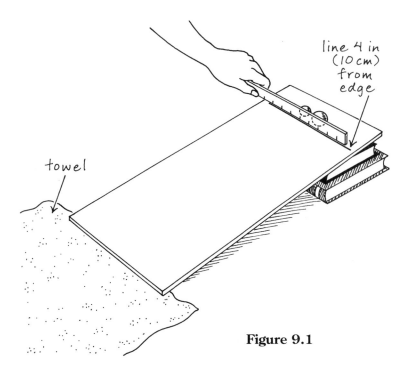

line 4 in (10 cm) from edge

towel

Figure 9.1

Results

The marbles reach the end of the ramp at the same time.

Why?

Energy is the capacity to move something. In other words it is the ability to do work. **Potential energy (PE)** is the stored energy of an object due to its position or condition. Objects have potential energy when work is done on them, such as lifting an object or compressing a spring. Objects with potential energy have the potential to do work. In reference to an arbitrary position where the potential energy of an object is defined as zero, if the object is raised above this position it is said to have **gravitational potential energy. Kinetic energy (KE)** is the energy possessed by an object resulting from the motion of that object. Another way of describing the kinetic energy of an object is to consider how it moves. Kinetic energy of an object with **translational motion** (motion in which the center of mass of an object moves from one place to another) is **translational kinetic energy. Rotation** is the turning motion of objects about their axis, and the kinetic energy due to rotation is called **rotational kinetic energy.**

   Mechanical energy (E_m) is the energy of motion. It is the energy of an object that is moving or has the potential of moving. Total mechanical energy is the sum of the potential and kinetic energies of an object; thus, E_m = KE + PE. At the top of the ramp, both marbles have the same total mechanical energy. In a perfect condition in which there would be no loss of energy due to air resistance or any other frictional force acting on the marbles, the mechanical energy of the marbles would be conserved. This means that the maximum mechanical energy of each marble at the top of the ramp is equal to its maximum mechanical energy at the bottom of the ramp. At the top of the ramp, the KE of the marbles equals zero, so they have only gravitational potential energy, GPE. As they move down the ramp, their height decreases and their **rotational speed** (the speed of an object rotating about its axis) and **translational speed** (the speed of an object being moved from one place to another) increase; thus their KE increases and their PE decreases until at the bottom, ground zero, the PE equals zero. This relationship between PE and KE is called the **law of conservation of mechanical energy.** The fact that the glass marbles have different sizes yet reached the bottom of the ramp at the same time indicates that their size did not affect their mechanical energy.

Try New Approaches

How do the translational speeds compare for other shapes? Repeat the investigation using different shapes, such as the following:

- a **disk** (a solid cylinder), such as an unopened can of solid food (tomato soup or cranberry sauce), or a dowel
- a **hoop** (a hollow cylinder), such as an empty can with the ends removed, or a cardboard tube

   For each test, use two objects of the same shape but different sizes, such as two solid cylinders or two hoops.

Design Your Own Experiment

1a. In the original experiment, the spheres differ in mass and size but have the same translational speed. Design a way to test the effect of only one of these factors, such as mass, on translational speed. Make sure that the only difference between the two objects is their weight. (Note that on Earth, a change in weight is a change in mass, with their relationship being 454 grams/1 pound.) One way to do this is to use two food cans of equal size but different weight. (You can use small, empty plastic cylinders with removable lids that can be filled with different solid materials, such as clay or sugar.) Using the ramp and procedure in the original investigation, compare the translational speeds of the two containers.

b. Repeat the procedure using spheres of different radii but with the same mass, such as large glass spheres and small metal spheres of the same mass.

2. How do the translational speeds of similarly shaped but different-size objects compare on a level plane? Design a way to compare these translational speeds. One way is to use different sizes of marbles. Design a way to give the marbles an equal forward force, such as by placing them on a floor in front of a lightweight box. Then snap the backside of the box with your finger.

3a. Objects of comparable shapes will roll down an incline at the same translational speed. How do the translational speeds of different shapes compare? Design an experiment to compare the translational speeds of a solid sphere, a disk, and a hoop. One way is to roll all three at the same time and compare their translational speeds. Instead of measuring the translational speeds, you can rate them and compare one to another. For example, the translational speeds of the three objects can be 1, 2, or 3, with 1 being the least amount. Record the information in a Translational Speed Data table like Table 9.1.

Table 9.1 Translational Speed Data						
Shape	**Translational Speed**					
	Test 1	Test 2	Test 3	Test 4	Test 5	Average
(solid) sphere						
disk						
hoop						

b. How do your experimental data for the translational speeds of a solid sphere, a disk, and a hoop compare to the known values for each? Mathematically determine the translational speeds for each of the shapes using the equations in Table 9.2, then compare your calculated values to your experimental data. In each equation, v_t = translational speed, g = gravity (9.8 m/sec^2), and h = height of the ramp measured in meters.

Table 9.2 Translational Speed Formulas	
Shape	**Formula, v_t = translational speed ($^m/_{sec}$)**
sphere (solid)	$v_t = 1.2\sqrt{gh}$
disk (solid cylinder)	$v_t = 1.15\sqrt{gh}$
hoop (hollow cylinder)	$v_t = \sqrt{gh}$

4. How does the distribution of mass about the axis of an object rotating down an incline affect its translational speed? Design a way to determine the effect of the location of mass on rotational kinetic energy. One way is to place weights at different distances from the object's axis. For example, use two identical cans with removable

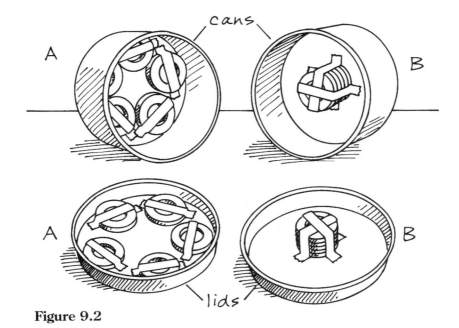

Figure 9.2

lids. Use a thin strip of duct tape to secure five metal washers around the inside rim of the bottom of one can and five washers around the inside rim of its lid. Stack and tape five washers together and use duct tape to secure them in the center of the bottom of the other can. Stack and secure five more washers and attach them to the middle of the inside of that can's lid. Put the lids on both cans. Using the ramp and procedure from the original investigation, compare the translational speeds of the two cans.

Get the Facts

1. The formula for translational speed of different-shape objects rolling is algebraically determined from the formula for the total mechanical energy. The total mechanical energy of an object at a height above a zero reference is the sum of translational kinetic energy, rotational kinetic energy, and gravitational potential energy. What is the algebraic expression for each of these energies? For information, see a physics text such as John D. Cutnell, *Physics: Third Edition* (New York: Wiley, 1995), p. 226.

2. The translational speed of a rotating object depends on how much of its kinetic energy is used in turning the object. This is a measure of rotational kinetic energy, which is related to inertia. What is rotational inertia? What is the difference in the rotational inertia of the different shapes investigated in this chapter? For information about the rotational inertia of different shapes, see a physics text; Chapter 10, "Rotational Inertia," in this book; and Robert L. Lehrman, *Physics: The Easy Way* (Roslyn, N.Y.: Barron's, 1998), pp. 101, 132–133.

10 Rotational Inertia: Resistance to Change in Rotary Motion

Inertia refers to the tendency of an object to remain at rest or to resist any change in its state of motion unless acted on by an outside force. All objects, whether stationary or in motion, have inertia. Rotational inertia is the property of an object that resists any change in rotary motion, which is motion about the axis of an object.

In this project, you will measure the torque (turning effect) required to overcome an object's rotational inertia. You will determine the effect of the radius of an object on its rotational inertia. You will also determine the effect of the location of the center of mass on rotational inertia.

Getting Started

Purpose: To measure the torque required to overcome an object's rotational inertia.

Materials

1 roll of new adding machine tape
⅜-by-36-inch (0.94-by-90-cm) dowel
golf ball–size piece of modeling clay
20 to 25 small paper clips

Procedure

1. Place the roll of adding machine tape on the dowel. This will be roll A.

2. Divide the clay in half and use the two pieces to support the dowel on the backs of two chairs.

3. Clip one paper clip on the end of the paper strip. Straighten a second paper clip to form a hook, and attach it to the first paper clip on the paper strip, as shown in Figure 10.1.

4. Add one paper clip at a time to the hook until the paper starts to unroll. Record the number of paper clips required to make the roll begin to turn as the torque in a Rotational Inertia Data table like Table 10.1.

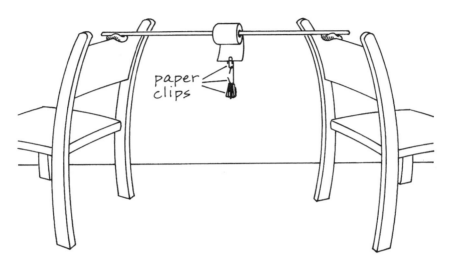

Figure 10.1

Table 10.1 Rotational Inertia Data						
Object	**Number of Paper Clips**					
	Trial 1	Trial 2	Trial 3	Trial 4	Trial 5	Average
Roll A						

Results

The number of paper clips will vary depending on different factors, including the size and weight of the paper roll. The roll used by the author required 18 paper clips.

Why?

Rotational inertia is the property of an object that resists any change in rotational motion (turning about an axis). If the rotational inertia of a stationary object is great, it takes a greater amount of torque to spin the object. **Torque** is the turning effort applied to an object that tends to make the object rotate. Torque is the product of a force and its perpendicular distance from a point about which it causes rotation to the axis of rotation. Just as a force applied to an object tends to change its translational motion, so a torque applied to an object tends to change the object's rotational motion. Since each paper clip applies a force on the paper roll at a perpendicular distance equal to the radius of the roll, each paper clip added increases the torque on the roll. The amount of torque needed to turn the paper roll indicates the magnitude of the roll's rotational inertia. Thus the more torque, indicated by the number of paper clips required to turn the roll, the greater is the rotational inertia of the roll.

Try New Approaches

How does the radius of an object affect its rotational inertia? Repeat the investigation using a second roll of tape with half the radius of the original one used. Add your findings to the Rotational Inertia Data table for this roll; called roll B. Note the radii of the two rolls.

Design Your Own Experiment

1. The **center of mass** of an object is the point at which the whole mass of an object is considered to be concentrated. This is the same as the center of gravity if the object is in a uniform gravitational field (the region of space in which a force of gravity acts on objects), such as that about Earth. The center of mass of a disk (a solid cylinder) is nearer its axis than is the center of mass of a hoop. Design an experiment to determine the effect of an object's center of mass in relation to its axis on the object's rotational inertia. Use objects with the same mass and shape but with different center-of-mass locations, such as two identical metal cans with lids and 10 metal washers. You will compare the rotational inertia of the cans by allowing them to roll down an incline. The can with the greater translational speed has less rotational inertia. Prepare the two cans by taping the washers inside (see Figure 9.2 on p. 64). Inside one of the cans, use thin strips of duct tape to secure five washers to the bottom of the can and five washers around the inside of the lid. In the second can, tape the five washers together in a pile and tape the pile to the center of the bottom of the can. Stack and secure five more washers and attach them to the middle of the inside of the can's lid. Put the lids on both cans. Place the cans together at the top of a ramp (this can be a board raised at one

end). Release the cans simultaneously and allow them to roll down the ramp. Use the results to decide how the location of the center of mass affects rotational inertia.

2. Another way to determine how the center of mass of an object affects its rotational inertia is to use two 36-inch (90-cm) dowels and four equal masses of clay. Add one clay mass to each end of one dowel. Hold the dowel in the center and rotate it back and forth for about half of a turn. Note the effort required to turn the dowel and to reverse the motion. In this position, the clay masses are each 18 inches (45 cm) from the center of the dowel, which is its axis of rotation, so the center of mass of the dowel is at its greatest distance from the axis. With the clay in this position, the rotational inertia will be called I_1. Place the remaining two clay masses around the second dowel at points 8 inches (20 cm) closer to the center of the dowel, which will be 10 inches (25 cm) from the center. In this position, the center of mass is closer to the axis. Rotate this dowel back and forth, as before, making a point to rotate it at the same speed as before. With the clay in this second position, rotational inertia will be called I_2. Repeat, rotating each dowel several times to make a comparison. As the rotational inertia of the dowel increases, it is more difficult to rotate it. Which dowel is easier to rotate? In other words, is I_1 greater than I_2?

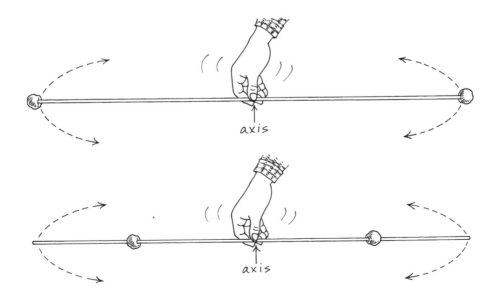

Figure 10.2

Get the Facts

1. Cats can quickly spin and land on their feet if dropped from an upside-down position. How is the rotational inertia of the front and the back of the cat changed? How does this difference affect the landing position? For information, see P. Erik Gundersen, *The Handy Physics Answer Book* (Detroit: Visible Ink, 1999), pp. 75–76. *Note:* It is not suggested that you try this with a cat. It takes special photographic equipment to make the observation, and special care must be taken to keep the cat from being injured.

2. *Newton's law of conservation of momentum* states that an object in motion remains in motion unless it is acted upon by a net force. This means that a rotating object will continue to spin unless it is acted on by a twisting force in the opposite direction. How is angular momentum determined? How can conservation of angular momentum be used to explain why a skater spins faster when the skater suddenly draws his or her arms in? For information, see Paul Doherty, *The Spinning Blackboard & Other Dynamic Experiments on Force & Motion* (New York: Wiley, 1996), pp. 55–58.

11 Pendulum: A Harmonic Oscillator

A pendulum is a weight hung so that it swings about a fixed pivot (a point about which something rotates). Because of the regularity of a pendulum's swing, it is a common timekeeping mechanism.

In this project, you will determine a simple pendulum's period (time of a back-and-forth swing). You will investigate the effects of the weight and the length of the pendulum on its period. You will also use a simple pendulum to determine the acceleration of gravity and discover why the angle of displacement of a pendulum has to be small to produce simple harmonic motion.

Getting Started

Purpose To determine the period of a simple pendulum.

Materials
24-inch (60-cm) string
metal washer
transparent tape
protractor
stopwatch

Procedure

1. Tie the string to the washer.

2. Tape the protractor to the edge of a table as shown in Figure 11.1.

3. Tape the string to the table so that the string falls across the center of the protractor.

4. Allow the pendulum to hang undisturbed. This vertical position is its resting position, labeled B in the figure. Then pull the washer to one side so that the string is at a 15° angle from vertical (position A). Release the washer and simultaneously start the stopwatch.

5. Record the time required for the washer to complete ten oscillations. Note that an oscillation is a back-and-forth swing from the displaced position A to C and back to A, indicated by arrows from A to C and from C to A.

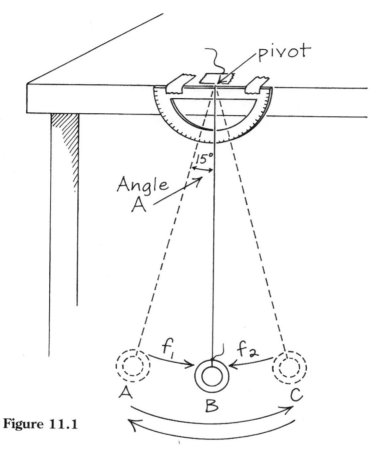

Figure 11.1

6. Determine the period by dividing the time by 10. Record this in a Pendulum Data table like Table 11.1.

7. Repeat steps 4 through 6 four times. Average the results.

Table 11.1 Pendulum Data						
Number of Washers	**Period, *T* (seconds)**					
	Trial 1	Trial 2	Trial 3	Trial 4	Trial 5	Average
1						

Results

You will have determined the period for the pendulum used.

Why?

A **pendulum** is a weight hung so that it swings about a fixed **pivot** (a point about which something rotates). A **simple pendulum** is a mass called a **bob** supported by a material, such as a string or wire of negligible mass hanging from a pivot. When a pendulum hangs vertical so that its center of gravity is below the pivot, it experiences zero net force (the sum of all forces simultaneously acting on an object) and is said to be at its resting point or in a stable equilibrium (position B in Figure 11.1). When the bob is pulled to one side, it is displaced an angular distance that depends on the amplitude of the pendulum. **Displacement** is the specific distance an object is moved in a specific direction. **Amplitude** is the farthest displacement of an object from equilibrium—the resting position for the pendulum. In this experiment the **displacement angle** (the angle the pendulum has moved from its resting position) is equal to 15° (angle A in Figure 11.1). The weight of the pendulum produces a **restoring torque** (the turning effect that reduces a pendulum's displacement angle) that moves the pendulum back toward its resting position. In Figure 11.1, f_1 and f_2 represent the restoring forces due to the pendulum's weight. When the pendulum is released, it exhibits periodic motion. For a pendulum, this means that it swings back and forth from position A to C and back to A about its resting position in a repetitive motion called an oscillation. The pendulum's period, T, is the time required to complete one oscillation.

At an angle of 15° or less, the periodic motion of the pendulum is considered to be **simple harmonic motion (SHM),** a condition in which the restoring torque is proportional to the displacement angle. This means that the restoring torque increases as the displacement angle increases. With simple harmonic motion, the period of a pendulum does not depend on amplitude.

Try New Approaches

1. How does the mass of the simple pendulum affect its period? Repeat the experiment four times, increasing the number of washers by one with each investigation. Record your results in a Pendulum: Mass vs. Period Data table like Table 11.2. **Science Fair Hint:** Display a photograph of the pendulum with a data table showing the average period for each mass.

Table 11.2 Pendulum Mass vs. Period Data						
Number of Washers	**Period, T (seconds)**					
	Trial 1	Trial 2	Trial 3	Trial 4	Trial 5	Average
1						
2						
3						
4						
5						

2. How does the length of the pendulum affect its period? Repeat the original experiment using different lengths of string. **Science Fair Hint:** Display a photograph of the pendulum with a Pendulum Period vs. Length Data table.

Design Your Own Experiment

1a. Gravity is the force that causes a pendulum to oscillate. As the pendulum moves down from its displaced position, it accelerates; as it rises, it decelerates. The relationship between the period and length of a pendulum and gravity is:

$$g = 4\pi^2 \, l/T^2$$

where g is the acceleration of gravity, l is the length of the pendulum, and T is the period of the pendulum. Design an experiment that uses a pendulum to determine the acceleration of gravity. One way is to build a support for the pendulum that is free-standing, such as the wooden stand in Figure 11.2. The pendulum can be a string with one or more washers attached. Measure and record the length of the pendulum (which is the length from where the string is attached to the pivot to the bob's center of gravity, generally its geometric center), and use the procedure from the original experiment to determine the pendulum's period. Use the equation to calculate the acceleration of gravity. Perform the experiment five times, recording your data in a Pendulum Acceleration Data table like Table 11.3. For more information, see Karl F. Kuhn, *Basic Physics: A Self-Teaching Guide* (New York: Wiley, 1996), pp. 104–105.

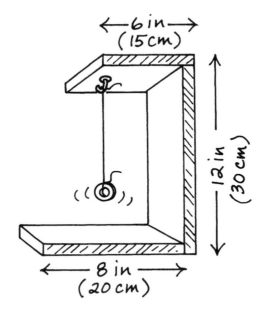

Figure 11.2

Table 11.3 Pendulum Acceleration Data			
Trial	Period (T), sec	Length (l), m	Acceleration of Gravity, m/sec²
1			
2			
3			
4			
5			
average			

b. The accepted value for the acceleration of gravity on Earth is 9.8 m/sec². Use the average acceleration of gravity to determine the relative error in your investigation. See Appendix 2 for information on determining relative error.

Get the Facts

1. A rigid pendulum, such as that in a clock, is called a *physical pendulum*. How does the period of a physical pendulum compare to that of a simple pendulum? For information, see Robert Ehrlich, *Why Toast Lands Jelly-Side Down* (Princeton, N.J.: Princeton University Press, 1997), pp. 123–124.

2. French scientist Jean Foucault (1819–1868) used a simple pendulum to demonstrate that Earth rotates on its axis. How did Foucault's pendulum prove that Earth rotates? For information, see Marc Alan Rosner, *Scientific American Great Science Fair Projects* (New York: Wiley, 2000), p. 115.

PART II

Fluids

12 Buoyancy: Upward Force by Fluids

Buoyancy is the upward force of a fluid on an object placed in it. Archimedes, a Greek mathematician, is given credit for explaining the force, called buoyancy, that supports objects in a fluid. Floating is usually associated with water, but floating can describe any object that is suspended in any other fluid—liquid or gas.

In this project, you will measure the buoyancy on a floating object by measuring the weight of water displaced (pushed aside) by the object. You will measure the difference between the weight of an object in air and the weight of the same object submerged in water, and compare the difference to the buoyancy of the water on the object. You will also investigate the relationship between the density of a fluid and its buoyancy.

Getting Started

Purpose: To measure the weight of water displaced by an object placed in it.

Materials
scissors
empty plastic 2-liter soda bottle
one-hole paper punch
flexible drinking straw
metric measuring cup (250 ml)
pitcher
tap water
3-ounce (90-ml) paper cup
20 pennies

Procedure
1. Cut the top section off the soda bottle. Discard the top and keep the bottom of the bottle.

2. Use the paper punch to make a hole in the plastic about 2 inches (5 cm) from the rim of the bottle.

3. Insert the short end of the straw into the hole so that the straw forms a 90° angle. Place the measuring cup under the free end of the straw.

4. Use the pitcher to pour water into the bottle until it is just above the straw. Water will then flow through the straw and into the measuring cup.

5. When the water stops flowing into the measuring cup, empty the cup. Replace the empty measuring cup under the straw.

6. Set the paper cup on the surface of the water in the bottle. Support the paper cup as you add the coins to the paper cup one at a time. Do not let water spill over the rim of the bottle.

Figure 12.1

7. When the water stops flowing through the straw into the measuring cup, remove the paper cup from the bottle. Record the volume of water in the measuring cup in **liters (L)** (an SI unit for volume).

8. Use the following equation to determine the mass of the water in kg:

$$m_{water} = D_{water} \times V_{water}$$

Where:

m = mass measured in kg
D_{water} = density of water, which is 1 kg/L
V_{water} = volume of water displaced in liters (L)

Example:
If the paper cup displaced 15 ml of water, which is equal to 0.015 L, then the mass of the water would be:

$$m_{water} = D_{water} \times V_{water}$$
$$= 1 \text{ kg/L} \times 0.015 \text{ L}$$
$$= 0.015 \text{ kg}$$

9. Use the following equation to determine the weight of the water in newtons (N).

$$F_{wt} = m \times g$$
F_{wt} = weight of water measured in newton units
m = mass of water in kg
g = acceleration of gravity, which is 9.8 m/sec^2

Example:
If 0.015 L of water is displaced, the mass of the water is 0.015 kg, and the weight of the water in newtons is:

$$F_{wt} = m \times g$$
$$= 0.015 \text{ kg} \times 9.8 \text{ m/sec}^2$$
$$= 0.147 \text{ kg·m/sec}^2$$
$$= 0.147 \text{ N}$$

Note: 1 newton = 1 kg·m/sec^2, so the weight of the water is 0.147 N.

Results

The paper cup floats in the water. The water pushed out by the paper cup spills over into the measuring cup. You used this volume of water to calculate the buoyancy of the paper cup. For the example, an object that displaces 0.015 L of water has a buoyancy of 0.147 N.

Why?

The paper cup floats in the water, with about half of the paper cup below the surface of the water. The paper cup **displaced** (pushed aside) the amount of water equal to the volume of the paper cup below the water's surface. **Buoyancy** is the upward force of a **fluid** (a substance, a gas, or liquid, that flows and offers little resistance to a change in its shape when under pressure) on an object placed in it. The buoyancy of the water on the paper cup equals the weight of the water displaced by the paper cup. The Greek mathematician Archimedes (298–212 B.C.) is credited with discovering the law of buoyancy, which states that any object submerged or floating in a fluid is buoyed (lifted) by a force equal to the weight of the fluid displaced. Once you know the amount of water displaced, you can calculate the weight of the water displaced, which is equal to the buoyancy in newtons.

Try New Approaches

1. An object will float as long as its weight is equal to the weight of water it displaces. Compare the weight of the cup and coins with the weight of the water it displaces determined from the original experiment. Determine the weight of the cup and coins by using a food scale to measure the mass of the cup and the coins in grams. Then convert the gram measure to kilograms and use the equation $F_{wt} = m \times g$ to determine the weight of the cup and coins in newtons.

2. What is the maximum weight at which the paper cup and its contents can remain afloat? Repeat the original experiment placing the paper cup in the water. As you add one coin at a time, make note of any change of position of the cup in the water. Continue to add coins until one more coin makes the paper cup sink. Remove one coin, then determine the weight of the dry cup and coins as before. Determine the weight of the water displaced by the cup. How do the two weights compare?

Design Your Own Experiment

1a. If Archimedes' principle is correct, buoyancy on an object in water causes the object to have an apparent weight (F_A) equal to the actual weight (F_{wt}) of the object as measured in air minus the weight of the water displaced by the object (F_B), which is equal to buoyancy. An equation that expresses this relationship is: $F_A = (F_{wt}) - (F_B)$.

Design a way to test this. One way is to determine the actual weight of a rock in air (F_{wt}) in newtons. Do this by using the previous method of measuring the mass of the rock on a food scale in kg, then calculate the weight using the equation $F_{wt} = m \times g$. Record the rock's weight (F_w) in a Buoyancy Data table like Table 12.1. Repeat the original experiment to determine the weight of the displaced water (F_B) when the rock is placed in water. Record the weight (F_B) in the data table. Calculate the apparent weight (F_A) of the rock using the equation $F_A = (F_{wt}) - (F_B)$ and record the results in the data table.

Table 12.1 Buoyancy Data			
Object	**Weight in Air (F_{wt}), N**	**Weight of Displaced Water (F_B), N**	**Apparent Weight (F_A), N**
Rock			

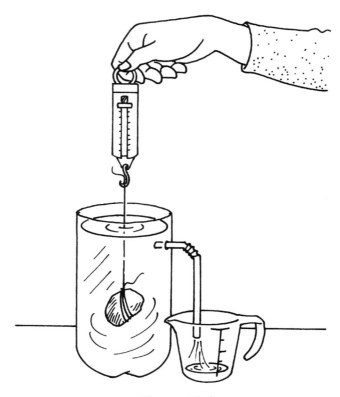

Figure 12.2

b. If two items of identical volume but different weights are submerged in water, would the buoyancy on each be the same? Design a way to determine this, such as by using a container that can be closed. Fill the container with different contents to change its weight.

c. How does the density of the fluid affect its buoyancy? Repeat the investigation using fluids with different densities, such as different concentrations of salt water. Since the density differences between the fluid concentrations may be slight, determine the densities by asking your teacher or maybe a pharmacist to measure the mass of a certain volume of each fluid on a scale accurate to at least 0.01 g. For more information about how things float, see Robert L. Lehrman, *Physics the Easy Way* (Hauppauge, N.Y.: Barron's, 1998), pp. 158–159.

Get the Facts

1. Most fish are able to remain suspended at depths beneath the surface of the water. They remain stable due to a condition known as *neutral buoyancy*. What forces create neutral buoyancy? How is a fish able to maintain neutral buoyancy? For information, see Mary and Geoff Jones, *Physics* (New York: Cambridge University Press, 1997), p. 56.

2. Air is a very light fluid with a density of only 1.25×10^{-3} g/ml (1.25 kg/m³). A few things, such as a balloon filled with helium or hot air, are light enough to float in air. Why can a balloon filled with hot air float in air? What is the flight ceiling for a hot-air balloon? For information, see Louis A. Bloomfield, *How Things Work: The Physics of Everyday Life* (New York: Wiley, 1997), pp. 128–134.

13 Atmospheric Pressure: Air Force per Area

A fluid is any substance, a gas or liquid, that flows and offers little resistance to a change in its shape when under pressure. Earth's atmosphere (the blanket of gases surrounding Earth) is made up of air, which is a fluid. Air has mass and weight, but no fixed size or shape. It is compressible, which means that the particles that make up air can be pushed closer together. The closer the particles are pushed together, the greater their density (amount of particles in a given volume). Pressure is the force exerted on a unit area of a surface. The measure of the force that results from the collision of air molecules in Earth's atmosphere on a specific area is called atmospheric pressure.

In this project, you will determine the affect of temperature on air pressure. You will also use a manometer to determine the direction of atmospheric pressure, and you will compare air pressures at different layers of Earth's atmosphere.

Getting Started

Purpose: To determine how a decrease in temperature affects air pressure.

Materials

1 plastic shoe box
cold tap water
12 or more ice cubes
black permanent marker
2 empty 1-liter plastic soda bottles
two 9-inch (22.5-cm) balloons
timer
5-ounce (150-ml) paper cup

Procedure

1. Fill the box half full with cold tap water.

85

2. Add the ice cubes to the water.

3. Use the marker to label the bottles A and B.

4. Place one of the balloons over the mouth of each bottle.

5. Stand bottle A next to the shoe box and lay bottle B on its side inside the box.

6. Use the paper cup to dip and pour the chilled water over the surface of bottle B for two or more minutes.

7. Observe the balloons on both bottles periodically, noting any changes in their size, shape, or position.

Figure 13.1

Results

There are no noticeable changes in the balloon on bottle A. The balloon on bottle B may be slightly less inflated, but basically there is no noticeable change in its size and shape. However, the balloon was partially moved inside bottle B.

Why?

Temperature is how hot or cold an object is, which is determined by the average kinetic energy (KE) of the particles of the object. When bottle B was chilled with the cold water, the temperature of the air inside the bottle decreased; thus the kinetic energy of the air particles inside the bottle decreased. With lower kinetic energy, the air particles move slower and there are fewer collisions of the air molecules on the inside surface of the bottle and balloon. Thus the **pressure** (the measure of the force exerted on a specific area) of the air inside bottle B decreased.

The number of air molecules inside the two bottles is the same. The temperature of the air outside bottles A and B is relatively the same, with a slight decrease of air temperature near bottle B due to the icy water. Thus the atmospheric pressure outside each of the bottles is relatively the same. **Atmospheric pressure** is the measure of the force of air on a specific area resulting from the collision of gas molecules in Earth's atmosphere on that area; also called **barometric pressure.** The atmospheric pressure outside bottle A and the pressure of the air inside the bottle are relatively the same; thus no change in the balloon is observed. But the atmospheric pressure outside bottle B is greater than the pressure of the air inside bottle B; thus the air molecules outside the bottle that collide with the surface of the balloon on bottle B push the balloon inside the bottle but the pressure is not enough to inflate the balloon.

Try New Approaches

Heating a gas causes its molecules to speed up, thus increasing the KE of the gas. How does this affect air pressure? Determine the effect that heating has on the air pressure by repeating the experiment using warm tap water in the shoe box. **Science Fair Hint:** Take photographs to indicate the size, the shape, and the position of the balloons at the start and finish of the experiment.

Design Your Own Experiment

1a. Earth's atmosphere is held in place around Earth by gravity. Atmospheric pressure, which is created by air molecules hitting and bouncing off of surfaces, including each other, keeps gravity from pulling all of the air molecules to Earth's surface. Gravity pulls the atmosphere downward, and air pressure pushes the atmosphere upward. Does this mean that atmospheric pressure is *only* directed upward against the pull of gravity? Design an experiment to determine the direction of atmospheric pressure. One way is to use a **manometer** (an instrument used to measure the pressure of fluids). See Appendix 3 for instructions on how to make a manometer. Test atmospheric pressure by holding one end of the manometer tube in different directions: right, left, up, and down. The water levels in the tubes will be even if the pressure on both sides is equal.

b. The weight of the column of air above an area of Earth at a lower elevation produces a greater atmospheric pressure than at a higher elevation. This is because as the column of air increases in height, its weight increases, causing the air molecules near Earth's surface to have greater density. As the density of air increases, the number of molecules of air hitting against a surface increases. Design an experiment to prove that atmospheric pressure is the same no matter where it is measured as long as the density of the air is the same. The manometer could be used to compare the atmospheric pressure of different air samples. One way is to stand the manometer outdoors, in a spot where only the atmosphere is above the instrument. Cut a notch out of one side of the lid of a box, such as a large shoe box. Set the box next to the manometer for one or more minutes so that the box will fill with the same air around the instrument. Insert the end of the manometer into the box and secure it to the inside of the box with tape. Close the box so the manometer tube fits in the cutout of the lid. Use tape to cover the opening in the lid around the tube. Compare the water levels in the tubes. Repeat with air collected from other places. Remember that temperature affects the density of air. If possible, repeat this experiment at different elevations, such as on a mountain and at sea level.

Figure 13.2

c. A diagram can be used to show how weight (measurement of the gravity force) and air pressure affect the structure of Earth's atmosphere. Show a 1-m-square column of the atmosphere made of blocks of an equal number of air molecules. Extending from Earth's surface, one block of air would be stacked on another. The air pressure of the moving air molecules of the bottom block would support the weight of all the blocks above it. The weight of the air blocks would tightly compress the air molecules in the bottom block, thus the bottom block would be more compressed (pushed together). Thus the density of this block would be greater than any above it. Near Earth's surface, the density of air is greatest, and atmospheric pressure is about 14.6 psi (pounds per square inch), which is about 100,000 Pa (pascals). At 3.4 miles (5.5 km) above Earth's surface, the pressure is about half that at Earth's surface; at 6.8 miles (11 km), the pressure is about a fourth that at Earth's surface. For more about the relationships among gravity, density, and air pressure, see Louis A. Bloomfield, *How Things Work: The Physics of Everyday Life* (New York: Wiley, 1997), pp. 123–127.

Get the Facts

1. A *siphon* is generally a tube used to make liquid flow from a higher level to a lower level. What effect does atmospheric pressure have on the flow of liquid in a siphon? For information, see Lewis Carroll Einstein, *Thinking Physics* (San Francisco: Insight Press, 1995), pp. 204–205.

2. A *barometer* is an instrument used to measure atmospheric pressure. Italian mathematician and physicist Evangelista Torricelli (1608–1647) discovered the principle of a barometer in 1643. How can a barometer be made? How does it work? For information, see *Janice VanCleave's A+ Projects in Earth Science* (New York: Wiley, 1999), pp. 187–192.

14 Static Fluids: Fluids at Rest

The word "static" indicates no motion, and fluids are liquid or gaseous materials that can flow. Thus, "static fluids" is the study of the characteristics of liquids and gaseous materials that are at rest.

In this project you will experimentally compare air pressure in different directions at a given point. You will experimentally determine the relation between pressure and depth in a static liquid. You will also experimentally test Pascal's law, which states that pressure applied to an enclosed fluid is transmitted equally in all directions and to all parts of the enclosing vessel.

Getting Started

Purpose: To compare air pressure in different directions at a given point.

Materials

1 pint (500 ml) jar
tap water
1 index card
large bowl

Procedure

1. Fill the jar with water.

2. Cover the mouth of the jar with the card.

3. Hold the jar over the bowl.

4. With one hand over the card, invert the jar.

5. Carefully remove your hand from the card.

6. Keeping the mouth of the jar at relatively the same height, slowly rotate the jar through a complete circle, 360°, so that the mouth of the jar faces down, and then up, and then down again.

7. Observe the surface of the card over the jar.

Figure 14.1

Results

The card remains over the mouth of the jar through the entire rotation. The part of the card over the mouth of the jar has no noticeable change in its slight concave (curves inward) shape throughout the rotation.

Why?

The water around the mouth of the jar wets the paper, and cohesion (the force of attraction between like molecules) between the water molecules and **adhesion** (the force of attraction between unlike molecules) between the water molecules and paper molecules form a seal. But this seal alone is not enough to overcome the force of gravity. The **concave** (inward curve like the surface of a plate) shape of the card over the mouth of the jar indicates that the card is being pushed into the jar by an outside pressure. This force is atmospheric pressure.

At a given point in a fluid, such as air in the atmosphere, pressure exerted by the fluid acts at right angles at every point on a submerged object. The card stays in place over the mouth of the jar regardless of orientation, showing that air pressure is exerted on the card from all directions. In the same way, at a specific height above Earth, atmospheric pressure is the same on all sides of an object as indicated by no noticeable change in the concave shape of the paper covering.

Try New Approaches

1. Does the size of the jar affect the results? Repeat the investigation using jars of different sizes but with the same mouth size as the original jar.

2. Does the size of the mouth of the jar affect the results? Repeat the investigation using jars with the same size but with different mouth sizes.

Design Your Own Experiment

1. The relationship between the pressure of a liquid and the depth (height) of that liquid is expressed by the formula $P_{liquid} = Dgh$, where D is the density of the liquid, g is the acceleration due to gravity (9.8 m/sec^2), and h is the height of the liquid column above the point in question. For a specific fluid such as water, if the density of the water (1×10^3 kg/m^3) remains the same throughout and since gravity is relatively constant, the only variable is depth. Thus the pressure on the liquid is directly related to depth or height of liquid in the cup.

    Design a way to test this. One way is to fill a container with water and make holes of identical size in the container at various depths (see Figure 14.2). The length (L) of the stream of water spurting from each hole can be used to compare pressure. The greater the depth of the liquid, the greater the pressure. Use a tall paper cup and make a hole near the bottom with the point of a pencil. Put a piece of tape over the hole and fill the cup. Measure the height from the hole to the top of the water's surface. Record this as the depth of hole A in a Pressure Data table like Table 14.1. Use this height and the equation $P_{water} = Dgh$ to determine the pressure of water with a density of 1×10^3 kg/m^3 at the depth of hole A measured in meters.

Example: The pressure of water at a depth *(h)* of 0.03 m is:

$$P_{water} = Dgh$$

$$P_{water} = 1 \times 10^3 \text{ kg/m}^3 \times 9.8 \text{ m/s}^2 \times 0.03 \text{ m}$$

$$= 0.294 \text{ kg·m·m/m}^3\text{·s}^2$$

$$= 0.294 \times 10^3 \text{ N/m}^2$$

$$= 0.294 \text{ kPa}$$

Note that the units kg·m·m/m³·s² can be grouped forming kg·m/s²·m².

Since 1 kg·m/s² = 1N, then 0.294 kg·m·m/m³·s² = 0.294 × 10³ N/m², and since 1000 N/m² = 1 kPa, then 0.294 × 10³ N/m² = 0.294 kPa. Kilopascal (kPa) is a practical metric unit for measuring pressure, since pascal (Pa) is generally too small.

Elevate the cup on an inverted rectangular container at one end of a tray so that the hole points into the tray. Remove the tape, and mark where the water squirting out of the hole first lands. Measure the distance from the hole to this mark and record it as the length of the water stream for hole A. Repeat this procedure for two other holes, B and C, above hole A, making sure you open only one hole at a time and that all the holes are of equal size.

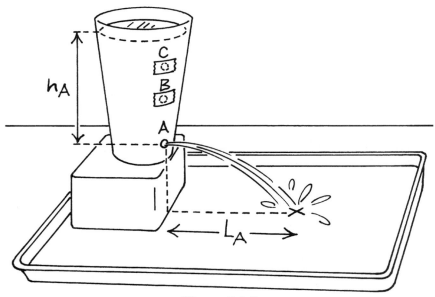

Figure 14.2

Table 14.1 Pressure Data			
	h = Depth of Hole (m)	Pressure (kPa)	L = Length of Water Stream (m)
hole A (bottom)			
hole B (middle)			
hole C (top)			

2. Blaise Pascal (1623–1662), a French mathematician and inventor, was the first to state that fluids at rest exert pressure equally in all directions. **Pascal's law** states that the pressure applied to an enclosed fluid is transmitted equally in all directions and to all parts of the enclosing vessel, if the fluid is incompressible. Design an experiment to test Pascal's law. One way is to squeeze a 2-liter plastic soda bottle containing water and a transparent condiment packet with an air bubble. The bubble of air in the condiment packet will increase or decrease depending on the pressure applied to it. When the bottle is squeezed, the liquid is not compressed but transmits the pressure in all directions, resulting in the compression of the air bubble inside the packet; thus the average density of the packet increases and the packet is less buoyant. Prepare the bottle by first selecting the best condiment packet. Do this by filling a quart (or liter) jar about three-fourths full of water and dropping several condiment packets into the water. Select the packet that just barely sinks below the water's surface. Insert the condiment packet into an empty 2-liter plastic soda bottle. Fill the bottle to overflowing with tap water. Secure the cap on the bottle. Then squeeze the bottle with your hands. The condiment packet will sink when the

Figure 14.3

bottle is squeezed and rise when the bottle is released. Note the size of the air bubble in the condiment packet as it sinks and rises. For more information about buoyancy, see Chapter 12, "Buoyancy: Upward Force by Fluids."

Get the Facts

1. In physics, pressure is force measured over an area. In the international system of units (SI), pressure is measured in newtons (N) per square meter. In honor of Pascal, the pascal (Pa) unit is used to measure pressure. There are other units of pressure, such as atmosphere, mm of mercury, bar, millibar, barye, and torr. Find out more about pascals and the other units of pressure. How do the other units compare to pascals? For information, see a physics text.

2. How does Pascal's law explain the workings of a hydraulic jack? For information, see Karl F. Kuhn, *Basic Physics* (New York: Wiley, 1996), pp. 75–76.

PART III

Electricity and Magnetism

15 Static Electricity: Stationary Charges

Electricity is the name given to any effect resulting from the existence of stationary or moving electric charges. The word "electricity" was coined by William Gilbert (1544–1603), an English physicist and physician known primarily for his original experiments on the nature of electricity and magnetism (phenomena associated with a magnet). Rubbing two materials together, such as your feet against a carpet, causes two kinds of electric charges in the atoms that make up the materials to separate. A buildup of stationary charges is called a static charge. The effect of static charges is called static electricity. If enough charges separate, a spark called static discharge is produced when the charges recombine. American scientist and statesman Benjamin Franklin (1706–1790) named the two kinds of charges "positive" and "negative." He also experimentally demonstrated that lightning, like the small spark created when you touch a metal doorknob after rubbing your feet on a carpet, is an example of static discharge as a result of the loss of static charges.

In this project, you will discover how to polarize a material by electrostatic induction (separation of charges due to the presence of a charged object). You will learn how to charge a material by friction and conduction. You will also determine how the distance between charged materials affects the electric force between them.

Getting Started

Purpose To polarize a material by electrostatic induction.

Materials
2 Cheerios
two 12-inch (30-cm) pieces of string
transparent tape
metric ruler
9-inch (22.5-cm) round balloon
wool scarf
yardstick (meterstick)

Procedure

1. Prepare two pendulums by tying Cheerios to the ends of the strings.

2. Using tape, secure the free ends of the strings to the edge of a table. The strings should be far enough apart, about 1 cm, so that the Cheerios bobs hang freely and are near but not touching. Note the separation between the strings and bobs.

3. Inflate the balloon to the size of a large grapefruit, and tie a knot in its neck to close it.

4. Charge the balloon by rubbing it with the wool scarf five or more times.

5. Hold the charged balloon under the hanging bobs so that the balloon is near but not touching them.

6. Slowly move the charged balloon to the left, then move it to the right. Observe the motion of the bobs.

7. Remove the balloon and place it at least 1 yard (1 m) from the bobs. Observe the position of the bobs in relation to each other for two or more minutes.

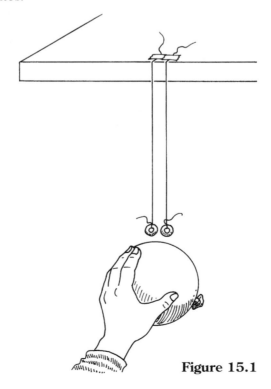

Figure 15.1

Results

At first the strings with bobs attached hang parallel to each other. As the balloon moves beneath the bobs, the bobs both move in the direction of the balloon's motion. Immediately after the balloon is removed, the strings hang at an angle to each other, with the bobs more separated than before. After a time, the strings return to the parallel position.

Why?

Electricity is any effect resulting from the presence of stationary or moving electric charges. A **charge (electric charge)** is the property of particles within atoms that causes the particles to **attract** (to pull together) or to **repel** (to push apart) one another or particles in other materials. The force between two objects due to their changes is called an **electric force.** The property of space around a charged object that causes forces on other charged objects is called an **electric field.** The source of positive and negative charges is **atoms** (the building blocks of matter), which contain a **nucleus** (the center part), with **protons** (positively charged particles inside the nucleus) and **electrons** (negatively charged particles outside the nucleus).

Physical contact between uncharged materials, such as rubbing objects together, is one method, called the **friction method,** of electrically charging them. Before the balloon and the wool were rubbed together, the balloon and the wool, like all materials, are **neutral** (having an equal number of positive and negative charges, thus having no electric charge). This is because they each had an equal number of protons (positive charges) and electrons (negative charges). When you rubbed the balloon with the wool, electrons were transferred from the wool to the balloon due to differences in attraction of the materials for electrons. An object with more of one kind of charge than another is said to be **charged.** The addition of electrons to the balloon gives the balloon a negative charge, and the loss of electrons by the scarf gives it a positive charge. The buildup of stationary electric charges is called **static charges.** The effect of static charges is called **static electricity.**

Two charged objects that have different kinds of charges attract each other, while two charged objects that have the same kinds of charge repel each other. So when the negatively charged balloon is brought near the neutral hanging Cheerios bobs, the positive and the negative charges in some of the molecules in the cereal separate slightly, because the negative charges are repelled by the negatively charged balloon. There is no increase in the net charge; there is only a redistribution of the charges. This redistribution gives the surface of the

Cheerios a slight positive charge. This process of **polarizing** (separating positive and negative charges) a neutral material due to the proximity (nearness) of a charged object is called **electrostatic induction** (see Figure 15.2).

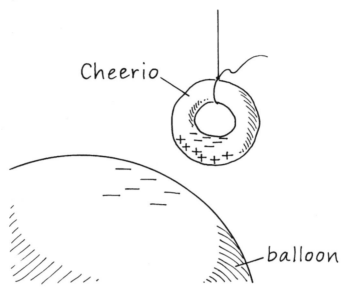

Figure 15.2

The positively charged side of the polarized bobs are attracted to the negatively charged balloon and move in the direction the balloon moves. When the charged balloon is removed, however, the now positively charged surfaces of the bobs repel each other, and they separate. But the induced positive charge is temporary, so when the charged balloon is no longer nearby, in a short time the separated charges return to their previous positions and the surfaces of the bobs become neutral and no longer repel one another. Thus the bobs hang straight down.

Try New Approaches

1. Does the material from which the bobs are made affect the time they stay charged after the balloon is removed? Repeat the experiment using different materials, such as Styrofoam, cotton, and aluminum foil, to make the bobs.

2. How would using a positively charged object affect the results? Since the balloon attracted the electrons from the wool scarf, the scarf becomes positively charged. Repeat the original experiment, again rubbing the balloon with the scarf, but this time using the scarf instead of the balloon to charge the bobs.

Design Your Own Experiment

1a. Charging by conduction is the process of electrically charging a neutral body by touching it with a charged body. Design a way to charge a body by conduction. One way would be to use the procedure from the original experiment, but this time instead of just holding the charged balloon near the bobs, touch the charged balloon to the two bobs for 1 to 2 seconds. Determine the time it takes for the bobs to lose their static charge, which is called **static discharge.**

b. Does the type of material being charged affect the results of the conduction experiment? Repeat the previous experiment using different materials for the bob such as paper and/or cotton balls.

2a. Design an experiment to determine how distance between charged materials affects the repulsive force of like electrical charges. One way is to use charged transparent tape. First lay a ruler next to the edge of a table. Tear off one piece of tape about 5 inches (12.5 cm) long. Press 4 inches (10 cm) of the tape to the table, leaving the last inch of the tape to hang over the table's edge. Repeat, pressing a second piece of 5-inch tape to the table near the first piece of tape. Wrap the free end of one piece of tape clockwise around the pointed end of a pencil. Repeat, wrapping the other piece of tape counterclockwise around a pencil as shown in Figure 15.3. Then charge two pieces of tape by quickly raising the pencils, ripping both pieces of tape from the table. Immediately hold the pencils parallel to the table with the 4-inch (10-cm) piece of tape hanging down. Move the pencils so that one piece of tape is above each end of the ruler and the sticky sides of the tape are face to face. Keep the pencil with the tape above the

Table 15.1 Electrical Charge/Distance Data						
Tape Length	Attractive Distance between Tape, inches (cm)					
	Trial 1	Trial 2	Trial 3	Trial 4	Trial 5	Average
4 inches (10 cm)						
2 inches (5 cm)						
8 inches (20 cm)						

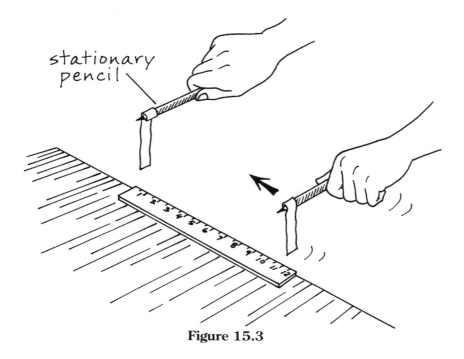

stationary
pencil

Figure 15.3

zero end of the ruler stationary, then slowly move the second pencil closer to the first one. Stop when there is any motion of the tape pieces, indicating repulsion of one piece to the other. Record the distance between the pencils in an Electrical Charge/Distance Data table like Table 15.1. Repeat this procedure four times. Average the results. Repeat, using different lengths of tape, such as 2 inches (5 cm) and 8 inches (20 cm). For more information about the effect of distance on electrical forces, see Larry Gonick and Art Huffman, *The Cartoon Guide to Physics* (New York: HarperPerennial, 1991), p. 108.

b. Repeat the experiment to determine if distance affects the attractive force between unlike charges. To produce unlike charges on the tape, first tear off one piece of transparent tape about 5 inches (12.5 cm) long. Wrap about 1 inch (2.5 cm) around the pointed end of a pencil. Lay the taped pencil on a table, with the smooth side of the tape against the surface. Wrap the end of a second 5-inch (12.5-cm)–long piece of tape around the pointed end of a second pencil. Place the sticky side of one of the tape strips against the smooth side of the other piece of tape. Holding the pencils, pull the tape apart. Immediately repeat the experiment, measuring the distance at which the attractive force between the tape is first observed.

Get the Facts

1. In 1785, French physicist Charles Coulomb (1736–1806) used a type of balance to measure the force between two charged spheres. Use a physics text to find out more about Coulomb's experiment and the equation he used to describe the relationships among electric forces, charge, and distance. This equation is called Coulomb's law. Another source of information is Karl F. Kuhn, *Basic Physics: A Self-Teaching Guide* (New York: Wiley, 1996), p. 139.

2. The triboelectric series ranks materials according to amount of energy needed to remove their electrons. For information about the triboelectric series, see Karl F. Kuhn, *Basic Physics: A Self-Teaching Guide* (New York: Wiley, 1996), p. 143.

16 Electric Current: Movement of Charges

Electricity is any effect resulting from the presence and/or movement of electrical charges. An electric current is the flow of electric charges. But the reason that an electric current makes a lamp come on instantly when you flip a switch is not because electrons race through the wire to the lamp. Instead, an electrical impulse, passed from electron to electron, moves through the wire to the lamp.

In this project, you will demonstrate the way an electrical impulse moves through a wire. You will determine how voltage affects an electric current. You will also investigate how to test the electrical conductivity or measure of the ability of a material to conduct an electric charge and the effect that the material's resistance has on an electric current passing through it.

Getting Started

Purpose: To demonstrate how an electrical impulse moves through a wire.

Materials
books
12-inch ruler
$\frac{1}{4} \times 16$-inch (.31 × 40-cm) dowel
four $1\frac{1}{8}$-inch (2.8-cm) ceramic disk magnets, each with a hole through the center

Procedure
1. Stack the books on a table so that you have two equal-size piles that are each at least $1\frac{1}{2}$ inches (3.75 cm) high.
2. Separate the stacks of books so that they are 12 inches (30 cm) apart. Lay the 12-inch ruler on the table between them.
3. Stick the dowel through the hole in one of the magnets.

4. Stick the dowel through the hole of a second magnet and push the two magnets on the dowel together. If the magnets cling together, remove the second magnet, turn it around, and put it back on the dowel. (The magnets are to push away from each other.)

5. Repeat step 4 twice, placing the remaining two magnets on the dowel.

6. Support the ends of the dowel on the edges of the books so that the magnets hang above the ruler. Place a book over the ends of the dowel to secure the dowel.

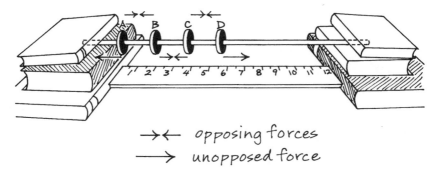

Figure 16.1

7. Push magnet D (see Figure 16.1) toward the zero end (the left side) of the ruler, which will force the rest of the magnets to move, until magnet A rests against the books and is above the zero end of the ruler. Slowly move your hand away from magnet D. Record the starting position of each of the magnets in a Magnet Movement Data table like Table 16.1. Magnet A's initial position is 0 inches (cm).

Table 16.1 Magnet Movement Data			
Magnet	**Position, inches (cm)**		**Distance Moved, inches (cm)**
	Initial	Final	
A	0	1(2.5)	1(2.5)
B			
C			
D			

8. Push magnet A slowly forward (to the right) 1 inch (2.5 cm).

9. While holding magnet A at its final position of 1 inch (2.5 cm), wait until all the magnets have finished moving, then measure and record the position of each of the magnets.

10. Determine how far each magnet moved by calculating the difference between the starting and the final position of each.

Results

Magnets B, C, and D appeared to move the instant that magnet A moved. Magnets B and C moved about the same distance as magnet A, which was 1 inch (2.5 cm). Magnet D moved farther than the others.

Why?

In this experiment the electrons in some solids, particularly metals, are attracted relatively equally to all nearby atoms and are not tightly bound to a single site. These electrons are relatively free to move through the solid, so they are called **free electrons.** The motion of free electrons results in the transfer of energy from one electron to the next. This transfer of energy is an **electrical impulse** caused by the repulsive force between negatively charged electrons. When magnet A was pushed forward, magnets B and C moved about the same distance because they each had about the same force pushing from their front and back. Thus they had the same net force acting in a forward direction. The magnets represent free electrons in a metal wire that is part of an **electric circuit** (the path that electric charges follow). An electric circuit is made of material called an **electrical conductor** or **conductor** (material with a large concentration of free electrons). If an electric circuit forms a loop so that the free electrons move in a continuous unbroken path, it is called a **closed circuit.** If there is a break in the materials forming the circuit so no current can flow, it is called an **open circuit.** There is no movement of charged particles in an open circuit. This experiment represents only a section of a closed circuit. Magnet D does not have a magnet in front of (i.e., to the right of) it, so it does not simulate the movement of an electron in a closed electric circuit. It moves farther than the rest of the magnets because it does not run into an opposing force, as do the others. (For more on the distance magnet D travels, see "Try New Approaches" in this chapter.)

Electricity is any effect resulting from the presence and/or movement of electrical charges. **Current electricity** is the result of moving electric charges. The flow of electric charges through a conductor is called an **electric current** or **current.** Energy associated with electricity is called **electrical energy.**

The electrical energy that causes an electric current to move can be compared to the stored potential energy of two opposing magnets in this experiment, such as magnets A and B. The closer the magnets are, the harder it is to push them together; thus as they move closer together, their potential energy increases. In like manner, the potential energy of two electrons increases when the two charges move closer together. The electrical energy needed to move a charge from one point to another in an electric circuit is called **potential difference** (difference in electric potential energy between two points).

In current electricity, the motion of the charges is very slow in comparison to the electrical impulse. Free electrons in a metal wire can wander from atom to atom through the metal. Imagine a single row of electrons in a wire. When electron A moves forward, electron B in front of it is pushed forward by the repulsive electrical force of their like charges. Electron C in front of electron B is then pushed forward by the repulsive electrical force, and so on, like the movement of the magnets in this experiment. While the individual electrons move at a speed of about 0.0004 inch (0.001 cm) per second, which is actually a great distance for such a small particle, the electrical impulse that they pass along moves almost as fast as light—186,000 miles (300,000 km) per second. In this experiment, while each magnet moves only a small distance, the magnet moves forward almost instantaneously, representing each transfer of electrical energy through a row of electrons (represented by magnets) by an electrical impulse.

Try New Approaches

The potential energy of a battery varies with the difference in the **volts** (the potential energy per charge) between the **terminals** (the points at which connections are made to an electrical device). This difference, called **voltage,** is the potential difference measured in **volts (V).** The greater the potential difference, the greater the potential energy, and therefore the greater the voltage. As the potential difference increases, the amount of current that flows through a circuit increases. A 1.5-volt battery tells you that the potential difference between the terminals is 1.5 volts. A 6-volt battery has four times more potential difference than a 1.5-volt battery. When connected to electric circuits, the 6-volt battery gives an electric charge four times as much push as the 1.5-volt battery.

Although an increase in voltage does not increase the speed of the electrical impulse, it does increase the speed of the electrons. As the speed of the electrons increases, more electrons move past a point in a given time period. Voltage can be thought of as a measure of the "push" on the free electrons. Demonstrate an increase in voltage by increasing the speed at which you move magnet A. Compare the distance that each magnet moves. Since magnet D doesn't have an opposing force, its movement is an indication of an increase in forward push.

Design Your Own Experiment

1a. **Electrical conduction** is the movement of electric charges through a substance. **Electrical conductivity** is the measure of the ability of a substance to conduct an electric current. Substances with high electrical conductivity are those with a large concentration of free electrons, such as metals, and are called **electrical conductors.** Design an experiment to compare the electrical conductivity of materials. One way is to build an open electric circuit so that different materials can be used to close the circuit. Place a 1.5-volt battery in a battery holder. Screw a flashlight lamp with an E-10 screw-base into a lamp holder. Use wire cutters to cut three 6-inch (15-cm) pieces of 22-gauge single-strand insulated wire. Strip about 1 inch (2.5 cm) of insulation from both ends of each piece of wire. Use the wire to connect the terminals of the lamp base and battery, as shown in Figure 16.2. Holding the insulated part of the wires, touch the free metal ends of the wires together to make sure the lamp will glow. If it does, separate the free ends of the wires and touch them to opposite sides of a testing material, such as a penny. *Note:* Make sure that the wires touch only the testing material and not each other. You want to determine if the testing material can close the circuit by allowing electrons to move through it, causing the lamp to glow. **CAUTION:** *The wires and the lamp can get hot enough to burn your skin if you leave the switch closed for longer than five seconds. Don't touch the lamp or the wires unless they have had time to cool after being disconnected.*

b. Some conductors restrict the movement of electric charges more than others. The measure of the opposition to the flow of electric charges through a conductor is called **resistance.** The brightness of the lamp is an indication of the amount of electric current (measure of the amount of electrical charges moving through a current per unit of time) in the circuit. As the resistance increases, the current decreases, and so does the brightness of the lamp. Repeat the previous experiment comparing the brightness of the lamp with each material. To be sure that the electrons travel through the same

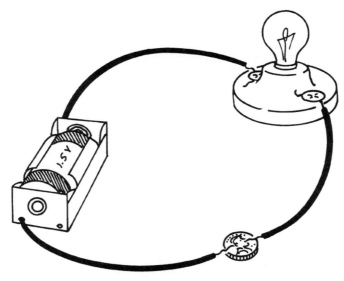

Figure 16.2

amount of testing material for each sample, tape the wires to a craft stick so that the metal ends stick out and are ½ inch (1.25 cm) apart (see Figure 16.3).

c. Design a way to determine if the amount of testing material affects the resistance. Use a longer sample, such as a strip of aluminum foil or pencil lead, and touch the wires to the testing material at different distances apart. (For information on using a multimeter to measure electric current, see chapter 17, "Series Circuit: Sequential Path.")

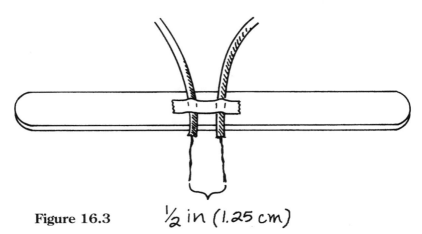

Figure 16.3   ½ in (1.25 cm)

Get the Facts

1. A *battery* is a device that uses chemicals to produce an electric current. By 1800, Italian physicist Alessandro Volta (1745–1827) developed what was called the voltaic pile, which was a forerunner of a battery. The voltaic pile was able to produce a steady stream of electricity. How does the voltaic pile compare to modern batteries? For more information about Volta's battery, see the Franklin Institute Science Museum, *The Ben Franklin Book of Easy and Incredible Experiments* (New York: Wiley, 1995), p. 56. You can find more information on the voltaic pile and its use in creating an electric current in Albert Einstein and Leopold Infeld, *The Evolution of Physics* (New York: Touchstone, 1966), pp. 84–90.

2. Coulomb's law describes the force between two charged objects. How does distance affect this force? For more about Coulomb's law, see a physics text.

3. An *electrical insulator* has a low concentration of free electrons and is a poor electrical conductor. Use a physics text to find out more about electrical insulators.

17 | Series Circuit: Sequential Path

An electrical circuit is the path that electric charges follow. When there is only one path through which an electric current can flow, the circuit is called a series circuit. If any part of a series circuit is broken, then no current can flow through any part of the circuit. Some holiday lights are in series circuits, so when one light burns out the circuit is broken and all the lights stop working.

In this project, you will use a model to demonstrate a series circuit. You will determine how to measure the voltage, current, and resistance of a series circuit. You will also learn how to determine resistance mathematically, using Ohm's law.

Getting Started

Purpose: To demonstrate a series circuit.

Materials

1.5-volt battery
battery holder with insulated wires (red and black)
flashlight lamp (for E-10 screw-base holder)
lamp holder with E-10 screw-base

Procedure

1. Place the battery in the battery holder so the battery's negative terminal is at the end with the holder's black wire.

2. Screw the lamp into the lamp holder.

3. Holding the insulated part of the wires attached to the battery holder, touch the bare ends of the wires to the screws on either side of the lamp holder (see Figure 17.1). **CAUTION:** *Do not leave the wires on the screws for more than a few seconds. The bare wire and lamp can get hot enough to burn you. Allow them to cool before touching them.*

4. Observe the lamp when only one wire leading from the negative terminal of the battery touches a screw on the lamp holder.

Figure 17.1

5. Repeat step 4 using only the wire from the positive terminal.

Results

The lamp glows only when the two wires leading from the battery touch the two screws on the lamp holder, one wire on either side of the lamp holder.

Why?

An electric current is the flow of electric charges. Electric current moves through conductors, such as the connecting wires from the battery holder and the metal parts of the lamp holder, lamp, and **battery** (a device that uses chemicals to produce an electric current). A path made of conducting materials through which an electric current travels is called an electric circuit. If the electric circuit is a loop, meaning a continuous path, it is called a closed circuit. If there is a separation of the conducting material forming the electric circuit, it is called an open circuit. If the circuit, like the one in this experiment, has only one path through which an electric current can flow, it is a **series circuit.**

The lamp indicated whether the circuit was open or closed. For the lamp to glow, electrons must move through its **filament,** which is a thin coil of wire inside the lamp. Because the filament wire is small, the electrons flowing through it are more likely to collide with atoms in the wire. These collisions cause the atoms to vibrate, thus increasing the temperature of the wire. When there is enough current, the wire heats enough to glow. When the circuit was closed, the wires attached to either side of the lamp led to each end of the battery allowing electrons to flow through the circuit, and the lamp glowed. An open circuit was formed when one of the wires from the lamp was removed from the battery. It made a break in the circuit, so the electrons could not flow. The light did not glow when the circuit was open.

The battery provides **direct current (DC)** (electric current moving in one direction). The arrows indicate that in a closed circuit, the current, indicated by the symbol e' in Figure 17.2, moves away from the negative terminal of the battery, through the lamp, and back to the positive terminal of the battery.

Try New Approaches

1. Would it affect the lamp's brightness if the electricity flowed in a reverse direction through the lamp? Repeat the experiment, rotating the battery holder 180° so that the positive (red wire) and negative (black wire) terminals are reversed.

2a. Would adding more lamps in the series circuit affect the brightness of each lamp? Repeat the original experiment, using two lamps in sequence. Use a 4-inch (10-cm) piece of 22-gauge wire to connect the lamp holders. Use wire cutters to strip a small section from each end of the wire and attach the bare wires to one screw on each of the lamp holders. **Science Fair Hint:** Use a schematic drawing, such as the one in Figure 17.2, to show a two-lamp series circuit.

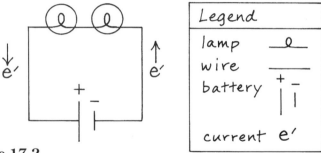

Figure 17.2

b. When lamps are connected in a series, what happens when one burns out? Determine this by unscrewing one of the lamps that is connected in series. (***Note:*** When a lamp burns out, the filament in the lamp breaks. Thus unscrewing the lamp gives the same effect as using a burned-out lamp.)

3. What effect does an increase in the number of batteries used have on the brightness of the bulbs? Repeat the original experiment, using one bulb and connecting two 1.5-V batteries in series by using a wire to join the negative terminal of one battery to the positive terminal of the other. **CAUTION:** *Use only 1.5-V batteries. Connecting more than two 1.5-volt batteries in a series or using batteries with a greater voltage may burn out the lamp as well as produce a dangerous amount of current.*

Design Your Own Experiment

1a. **Coulomb (C)** (charge on 6.25×18^{18} electrons) is the SI unit for quantity of electric charge. One coulomb per second is called an **ampere (A)** (unit measure of electric current), more commonly called **amps.** A device used to measure the amount of electric current in a circuit is called an **ammeter.** A **multitester** is an instrument that has the ability to work like a number of instruments, including an ammeter and a **voltmeter** (an instrument used to measure voltage). A multitester can be purchased at an electronics store. Design an experiment that uses a multitester as an ammeter to measure the current in any or all of the series circuits in the previous experiments. Follow the directions provided with your multitester, but note the information shown here for the multitester used by the author. **CAUTION:** *An ammeter is always connected in series. This means that when using the multitester to measure current, you must break the circuit being measured and make the ammeter part of the circuit. You can ruin the multitester if this is not done.* Figure 17.3 shows a diagram of a circuit with a battery, lamp, **switch** (device used to open and close an electric circuit), and ammeter. The author's multitester has a scale for measuring DC current from 0 to 150 mA (milliamps). To measure current, the function selector is set to 150 mA DC (see Figure 17.4). Attach the negative test lead (black) from the multitester to the negative side of the circuit and the positive test lead (red) to the positive side of the circuit, as shown in Figure 17.4. Only the DCV/mA part of the scale on a multitester is shown in Figure 17.4. While numbers are not printed on this scale, with the tester selector set to 150 mA DC, the fifteen long marks on the scale each measure 10 mA, which is read as 10 milliamps. The current reading for the circuit in Figure 17.4 shows the scale needle on the small mark between 30 mA and 40 mA; thus the current is 35 mA and is equal to 0.035A.

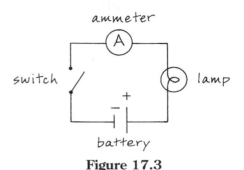

Figure 17.3

b. Does it matter where in the circuit the multitester is placed? Design series circuits and use the multitester to test in different places along the circuit, such as between two lamps or on the positive side of the battery and then on the negative side.

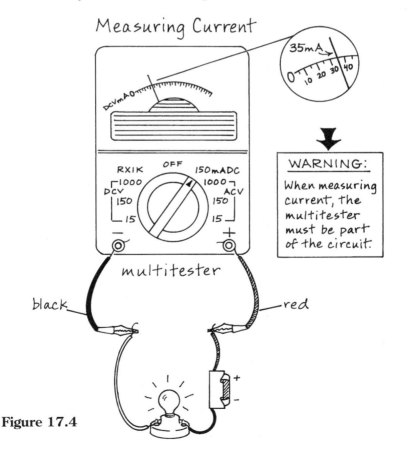

Figure 17.4

2. The driving force that pushes the electrons around the circuits in the experiments in this chapter is the battery, which acts like an electron pump. Voltage is a measure of the amount of potential energy that the battery transfers to electrons in a circuit. It is a measure of the difference in the energy on either side of the cell. The unit measure of voltage is volts (V). A multitester can act as a voltmeter. Design an experiment so that voltage can be measured. You may wish to place a switch in the circuit to make it easier to open and close the circuit. Use the multitester to measure the voltage in any or all of the series circuits in the previous experiments. Follow the directions provided with your multitester, but note the information shown here for the multitester used by the author. **CAUTION:** *A voltmeter should NEVER be part of a circuit; instead, it should be connected across a circuit.* Set the function selector to the lowest DC V position, which is 15 on the author's multitester. To determine the voltage through one of the lamps, touch the negative test lead (black) to the negative side of the circuit and the positive test lead (red) to the positive side of the circuit, as shown in Figure 17.5A. The voltage in the diagram is read as 1.5 volts. Figure 17.5B shows a schematic for the circuit with a voltmeter.

3. Each device in a circuit affects the flow of electrons, and some restrict the flow more than others. Any device in a circuit, such as a lamp and wire, offers resistance. But a device that is used to create electrical resistance in an electric circuit is called a **resistor.** Resistance is measured in the SI unit of **ohm (Ω).** A multitester can be used to measure resistance, but the resistance of the circuits in this chapter may be too low to be measured accurately by the tester. Instead, since the voltage and the current can be measured, the relationships among voltage, current, and resistance, known as **Ohm's law,** can be used to calculate resistance. This relationship is expressed as $V = I \times R$, which is read: V voltage (in volts) equals I, current (in amperes) times R, resistance (in ohms). If the voltage and the current are known, the resistance can be calculated using the following formula:

$$R = V \div I$$

For example, if a circuit has a voltage of 1.5 V and a 35 mA current, the resistance would be:

$$R = 1.5\text{ V} \div 0.035\text{ A}$$
$$= 42.85\ \Omega$$

For more information about Ohm's law, see Karl F. Kuhn, *Basic Physics: A Self-Teaching Guide* (New York: Wiley, 1996), pp. 152–153.

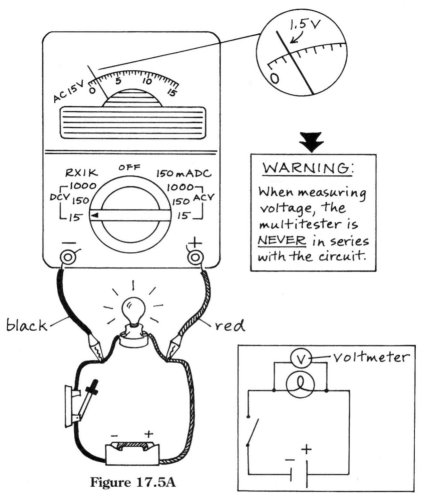

Figure 17.5A

Figure 17.5B

Get the Facts

A battery is made of one or more *electrical cells* connected in series. What are electrical cells made of? Is a flashlight battery technically a battery or a cell? How do electrical cells produce the driving force of the battery? What is a dry cell? What is the electric potential of a battery, and what causes it? For information, see physics texts as well as Mary and Geoff Jones, *Physics* (New York: Cambridge University Press, 1977), pp. 202–203.

18 Parallel Circuit: Divided Pathways

A parallel circuit is an electric circuit in which the electric current has more than one path to follow. The advantage is that, like adding another lane on a busy freeway, more traffic can flow. With a parallel circuit, more electric current can flow.

In this project, you will determine the path that electrons follow in a parallel circuit. You will measure the total current and voltage of each circuit as well as the connected branches, and you will use these measurements to confirm Ohm's law. You will also investigate how battery cells are connected in parallel and the effect of parallel cells on the current and voltage of a circuit.

Getting Started

Purpose: To determine the path of the electric current in a parallel circuit.

Materials

1.5-volt battery
battery holder with insulated wires (red and black)
2 identical flashlight lamps (for E-10 screw-base holder)
2 lamp holders with E-10 screw-base
wire cutter
12-inch (30-cm) piece of 22-gauge insulated wire
screwdriver with head type for lamp holder screws

Procedure

1. Place the battery in the battery holder.

2. Screw the lamps into the lamp holders.

3. Use the wire cutter to cut the wire into two 6-inch (15-cm) parts. Then strip about ½ inch (1.25 cm) of insulation from each end of the wires.

4. Attach the wires to connect the lamp holders, as shown in Figure 18.1.

5. Holding the insulated part of the wires attached to the battery holder, touch the bare ends of the wires to the screws on either side of one of the lamp holders, as shown in Figure 18.1. Compare the brightness of the lamps. **CAUTION:** *Do not leave the wires on the screws for more than 5 to 6 seconds. The bare wire and lamp can get hot enough to burn you. Allow them to cool before touching them.*

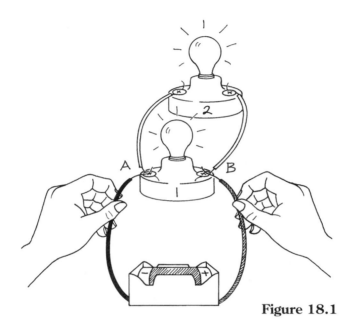

Figure 18.1

Results

The lamps glow with equal brightness.

Why?

The electric current has more than one path to follow through the connected lamps in this experiment, so the circuit formed what is called a **parallel circuit.** The arrows in the electrical schematic in Figure 18.2 indicate the movement of the current (e′) away from the negative terminal of the battery through the bulbs, then back to the positive terminal of the battery. At junction A (one of the screws on the side of lamp base 1), the current divides before moving through the lamps. Then the current recombines at junction B (one of the screws on the opposite side of lamp base 1) and returns to the positive terminal of the battery. The facts that the lamps are identical and glow with equal brightness show that the same amount of current reaches both lamps.

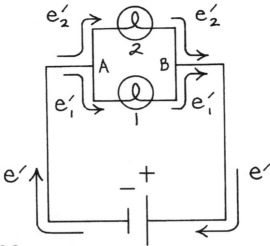

Figure 18.2

Try New Approaches

1. Would it affect the brightness of the lamps if more lamps were connected in parallel? Repeat the experiment, adding more lamps.

2. Would it affect the brightness of the lamps connected in parallel if a
lamp is placed in series with them? Repeat the original experiment,
connecting two lamps as in the original investigation and adding a
third lamp in series, as shown in the schematic in Figure 18.3.

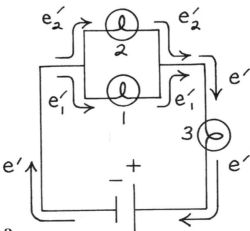

Figure 18.3

Design Your Own Experiment

1. Do the lamps in a parallel circuit have to be geometrically parallel to each other, or just connected so that the electrons have different paths from the negative side to the positive side of the battery? Design different electrical schematics, such as the one shown in Figure 18.4 Then assemble the circuits using the indicated lamps and battery for each schematic. Allow the brightness of the bulbs to indicate any change in the flow of the current through them.

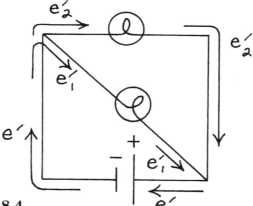

Figure 18.4

2a. Ohm's law describes the total current in a parallel circuit (I_t) as the sum of the currents in each branch of the circuit. Design a circuit with two or more lamps in parallel to confirm that for devices in parallel $I_t = I_1 + I_2 + I_N$. In the equation, I_t is the total current, I_1 is the current through lamp 1, I_2 is the current through lamp 2, and I_N represents the sum of other lamps in parallel, such as I_3, I_4, and so on. Use a multitester, such as the one described in Chapter 17, to measure the currents.

b. Ohm's law describes the voltage of lamps in parallel as the same as the total voltage of the circuit. Use the circuit in the previous experiment and the multitester to confirm that V_t (total voltage) + V_N (sum of voltage across other lamps in parallel) = V_1 (voltage across lamp 1) + V_2 (voltage across lamp 2). For more information about parallel circuits, see Karl F. Kuhn, *Basic Physics: Self-Teaching Guide* (New York: Wiley, 1996), pp. 152–158.

3. Battery cells in series are connected so that the **anode** (positive terminal) of one cell is connected to the **cathode** (negative terminal) of

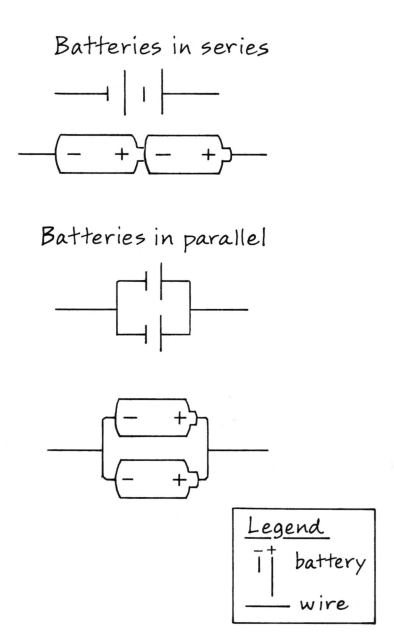

Figure 18.5

another cell. In parallel cells, like terminals are connected, anode to anode and cathode to cathode. Figure 18.5 shows two batteries connected in series and two batteries connected in parallel. Design an experiment to determine the effect of parallel cells on the current and voltage of a circuit. One way is to connect two batteries in parallel, then assemble a circuit with this parallel battery, a lamp, and a switch. **CAUTION:** *Use only 1.5-V batteries. Connecting more than two 1.5-volt batteries in a series or using batteries with a greater voltage may burn out the lamp as well as produce a dangerous amount of current.* For more information about batteries, see Mary and Geoff Jones, *Physics* (New York: Cambridge University Press, 1997), pp. 202–203.

Get the Facts

Christmas lights were at one time wired in series to save on cost, but most are now wired in parallel. What effect did a burned-out bulb have when the bulbs were in series? In parallel? Which is used in homes— series or parallel circuits? For information, see P. Erik Gundersen, *The Handy Physics Answer Book* (Detroit: Visible Ink, 1999), pp. 313–314.

19 Magnetic Field: An Area of Force

Magnetic force, a phenomena of magnetism, is a force produced by the motion of electric charges in a material. Materials with magnetic forces are called magnets, and the area around a magnet where its magnetic force can be experienced is called a magnetic field. One of the two regions of a magnet where the magnetic field is strongest is called a magnetic pole. One magnetic pole is called the north pole (N), and the other the south pole (S). Unlike poles attract each other, and like poles repel each other.

In this project, you will demonstrate how the angle of magnetic repulsive forces affects the motion of another magnet. You will discover how the magnitude of the repulsive force of one magnet affects the motion of another. You will determine how the strengths of magnetic fields can be compared. And you will study the effect of distance on the strength of magnetic fields.

Getting Started

Purpose: To demonstrate how the angle of magnetic repulsive forces affects the motion of another magnet.

Materials
ruler

pencil

1 sheet of copy paper

craft stick

transparent tape

3 equal-size disk ceramic magnets

compass

Procedure

1. Use the ruler and the pencil to draw a line down the center of the paper. Draw two additional lines 2 inches (5 cm) on either side of the center line on the paper.

2. Draw a line across the shorter center length of the craft stick and two additional lines 2 inches (5 cm) on either side of this center line. Repeat on the opposite side of the stick.

3. Determine the magnetic poles of the magnets by placing a compass on a wooden table and laying one of the disk magnets on the table about 12 inches (30 cm) from the compass and perpendicular to the compass needle. Slowly move the magnet toward the compass until the compass needle is attracted to the magnet. If the north end of the needle is attracted to the magnet, use the pencil to mark S on the top of the magnet. Turn the magnet over and mark N on its opposite side. If the needle's south end is attracted to the magnet, mark N on the magnet's top and S on its opposite side. Repeat this procedure for the other magnets.

4. Place two of the three magnets facedown on the two outside lines on the craft stick, with north poles (N) facing down. Tape the craft stick to the magnets.

5. Place the craft stick with magnet side down at the bottom of the paper so that the stick is parallel with the bottom of the paper and perpendicular to the lines on the paper. The center line on the craft stick should line up with the center line on the paper.

6. Place the unattached magnet (A) on the center line of the paper 2 inches (5 cm) from the craft stick. This magnet should have the north pole (N) facing up like the magnets taped to the stick.

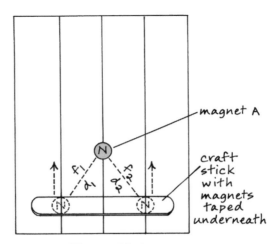

Figure 19.1

7. Slowly move the craft stick toward magnet A, making an effort to keep the lines on the stick matching up with the lines on the paper. Observe any movement of magnet A.

Results

As the craft stick approaches magnet A, the magnet moves away from the craft stick along the center line in a series of steps. It stops and then moves, then stops and moves, and so on.

Why?

Materials with a force called **magnetic force**—force produced by the motion of electric charges—are called **magnets,** and the area around a magnet where its magnetic force can be detected is called a **magnetic field.** All phenomena associated with magnets are called **magnetism.** Magnet A moves along the line due to a force between it and the magnets taped to the craft stick. Every magnet has two separated **magnetic poles** (region of a magnet where the magnetic forces appear strongest), called south and north poles. Near Earth's **North Pole** (the northernmost point on Earth) is a place called Earth's **magnetic north pole.** This is the place where the north pole of a free-swinging magnet such as the compass needle points. The south pole of the compass needle points to Earth's **magnetic south pole,** near Earth's **South Pole** (the southernmost point on Earth).

Unlike poles of two magnets attract, and like poles repel each other. All the magnets in the experiment are positioned so that like poles face each other. The magnets attached to the craft stick act as driving forces, causing magnet A to retreat. The movement of magnet A is along the center line, which bisects the angle formed by the lines from the magnets attached to the craft stick. The driving force is the result of the magnetic repulsive forces f_1 and f_2, from the two magnets acting at angles on magnet A. The stop-and-go movement of magnet A is due to the friction between the magnet and the paper. The driving force has to be strong enough to overcome the friction so that the magnet can move. The driving force weakens as the distances d_1 and d_2 increase until the magnet stops. Then, as the distances decrease, the driving force increases, and there is again enough force on magnet A to move it.

Try New Approaches

1. What effect, if any, does the angle of repulsive forces f_1 and f_2 have on the direction of the retreating magnet? Repeat the experiment twice.

First make the angles smaller, by making the distance between the center lines and the two lines on either side less than 2 inches (5 cm). Then make the angles greater, by making the distance greater than 2 inches (5 cm).

2. What effect would a difference in strength of the driving force have on the results? Repeat the original experiment, increasing the strength of one of the magnets by placing a third magnet on the craft stick. Place the magnet on top of the stick above one of the lower magnets, with unlike faces of the magnet toward each other. In this position the stacked magnets will attract each other, thus holding the magnet on this stick.

Design Your Own Experiment

1. Every magnet has an area of force around it that can affect other magnets. This area is called its magnetic field. Design an experiment to compare the strengths of magnetic fields. One way is to place a compass on a wooden table. When the compass needle comes to rest in line with Earth's magnetic field, slowly rotate the compass so that the north end of the needle points to N printed on the compass. The needle aligns itself so that it points to the north magnetic pole of Earth. Place a ruler next to the compass and perpendicular to the compass needle. Use one of the marked magnets from the original experiment. Lay the magnet with side N up at the end of the ruler so that it is 12 inches (30 cm) from the compass. Slowly move the magnet toward the compass, stopping when the compass needle is **deflected** (turned aside) 90° from N. Note the distance the magnet is from the compass. Repeat, using a magnet with a greater magnetic field strength, such as a stack of three disk magnets from the original experiment, with sides N up.

2. Design an experiment to determine how the distance from a magnet affects the strength of its magnetic field. One method is to draw two perpendicular lines across the center of a sheet of copy paper. Label the lines N, S and E, W, as shown in Figure 19.2. Use a ruler to mark 12 centimeters along line W, starting with zero at the compass. Place a compass where the lines cross. Rotate the compass so that the N on the compass lines up with line N. Place one of the labeled disk magnets (A) at the far end of line N with side S up. Move the magnet toward the compass until the north end of the compass needle points toward the magnet and is in line with line N. Place a second labeled disk magnet (B), of equal strength, with side S up at the far end of line

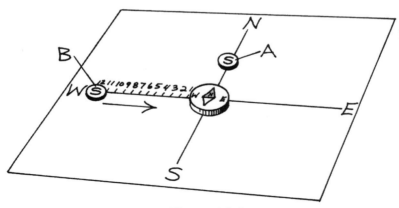

Figure 19.2

W. Move magnet B 1 cm at a time toward the compass. Record any deflection of the compass needle from north in a Magnetic Field Data table like Table 19.1. Use the relationship between distance and deflection angle in this experiment to determine the relationship between magnetic field strength and distance.

| Table 19.1 Magnetic Field Data ||
Distance from the Compass, cm	Deflection Angle, °
1	
2	
3	
4	
5	
12	

For more information about the relationship of distance and the strength of a magnetic field, see Robert Ehrlich, *Why Toast Lands Jelly-Side Down* (Princeton, N.J.: Princeton University Press, 1997), pp. 150–151.

3. Design a way to show that magnetic force fields of different magnets overlap. One way is to place four equal-size disk magnets facedown next to a metric ruler, with their north poles facing up. Use tape to secure the magnet nearest the zero end of the ruler. (See Figure 19.3.) Push the magnets as close together as possible. Compare the distance between the magnets, and explain how overlapping magnetic fields cause the differences between distances d_1, d_2 and d_3, and why f_1 is greater than any of the other forces, f_2 and f_3, between magnets.

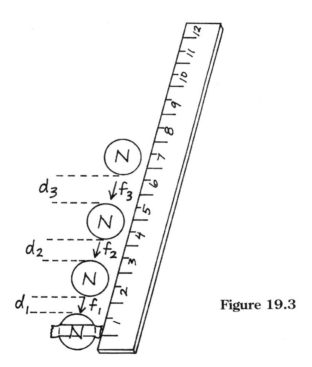

Figure 19.3

Get the Facts

1. A *line of flux* is a line drawn so that a tangent to it at any point indicates the direction of a magnetic field. What is magnetic flux density? For information, see Corinne Stockley, *The Usborne Illustrated Dictionary of Physics* (London: Usborne, 2000), p. 72.

2. *Ferromagnetism* is the property of a substance by which it is strongly attracted by a magnet. How does electron motion produce ferromagnetism? What is a domain? For information, see a physics text.

Electromagnetism: Magnetism from Electricity

In 1820, Danish physicist Hans Oersted (1777–1815) noticed that a compass needle was deflected at right angles to a wire carrying an electric current. Since a compass needle is deflected by a magnet, he concluded that the electric current somehow caused a magnetic field around the wire. Further studies by Oersted proved that any wire carrying an electric current has a magnetic field around it. Oersted's discovery started the study of electromagnetism (relationship between magnetic fields and electric currents) and the use of an electromagnet (device that uses an electric current to produce a concentrated magnetic field).

In this project, you will determine the direction of a magnetic field around a current-carrying wire. You will determine the effect of the direction of an electric current in a current-carrying wire on the pattern of the magnetic field around it. You will also make an electromagnet, determine its polarity, and test its strength.

Getting Started

Purpose: To determine the direction of a magnetic field around a current-carrying wire.

Materials

pencil
ruler
sheet of copy paper
compass
1.5-volt D battery
wire stripper
12-inch (30-cm) piece of 20- or 22-gauge insulated
    single-strand wire

Procedure

1. Use the pencil and the ruler to draw two perpendicular lines across the center of the paper. Label the longer line N, S and the shorter one E, W (as shown in Figure 20.1).

2. Place the paper on a wooden table and set the compass in the center of the paper, where the lines cross.

3. Allow the needle to come to rest in line with Earth's magnetic field.

4. First rotate the compass so that N on the compass is in line with the needle pointing north. Then lift the compass and rotate the paper so that its compass directions match those on the compass. Replace the compass on the paper.

5. Place the battery on the east side of the paper, with the negative terminal of the battery pointing south.

6. Using the wire stripper, remove about 1 inch (2.5 cm) of insulation from each end of the wire.

7. Bend the wire so that it has a straight center piece slightly wider than the battery's length.

8. Holding the insulated part of the end of the wire, position the wire so that the center section is about 1 inch (2.54 cm) above the compass and across the compass from north to south. Then touch the bare

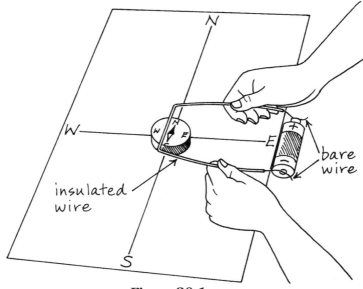

Figure 20.1

ends of the wire to the ends of the battery for about 1 second. Notice the direction in which the north end of the compass needle moves. **CAUTION:** *For your safety, hold the insulated part of the current-carrying wire so that you do not get burned or shocked. Holding the wires against the battery terminals for longer than 3 seconds can result in the wire becoming hot enough to burn your skin.*

Results

With the battery's negative terminal pointing south and the battery on the east side of the compass, the north end of the compass needle deflects from its north position toward the east.

Why?

The direction of the current in the wire is from the battery's negative terminal to its positive terminal. Current in the wire produces a magnetic field. With the current flowing in a south-to-north direction, the magnetic field below the wire is toward the east, as indicated by the deflection of the north end of the compass needle toward the east. The relationship between a magnetic field and an electric current is called **electromagnetism.**

Try New Approaches

1. What effect would moving the battery to the opposite (west) side of the compass have? With the negative terminal of the battery pointing south as before, repeat step 8 of the original experiment.
2. What effect would changing the direction of the current through the wire have on the deflection of the compass needle? Rotate the battery 180° so that the terminals of the battery have been reversed.

Design Your Own Experiment

1. A current-carrying straight wire is said to have a magnetic field encircling it. Design a way to show that the direction of the magnetic field is in a circle around a current-carrying straight wire. One way is to compare the direction of the magnetic field above and below the wire in the original experiment. Design a way to raise the compass and place the wire below it, such as by forming a stand for the compass by bending the ends of an index card.
2. A magnetic field is made up of imaginary lines called **magnetic field lines** that indicate the direction and magnitude of the field. Design a

way to show the pattern of the magnetic field lines around a magnet. One way is to place a piece of insulated wire through a piece of cardboard, such as the top of a small cardboard box. Sprinkle a thin layer of iron filings on the cardboard around the wire in a circle with about a 4-in (10-cm) diameter. Connect the ends of the wire to the terminals of a 1.5-volt battery. Observe the pattern of concentric circles (circles with a common center) around the wire. Repeat the procedure after rotating the battery 180° so the direction of the current is reversed.

3. An **electromagnet** is a device that uses electric current to produce a concentrated magnetic field. An electromagnet is made of a **solenoid** (coil of wire through which a current can pass) with a core of magnetic material such as iron. The current-carrying wire in a solenoid produces a magnetic field, which **magnetizes** (causes a substance to become a magnet) the iron core. Design an experiment to determine the **polarity** (the direction of the magnetic poles) of an electromagnet. One way is to wrap a 3-foot (90-cm) piece of 22-gauge insulated wire around a 16d finishing nail (also called a 16-penny nail) (see Figure 20.2). Leave about 4 inches (10 cm) of free wire at each end. Use a wire cutter to strip about 1 inch (2.5 cm) of insulation from

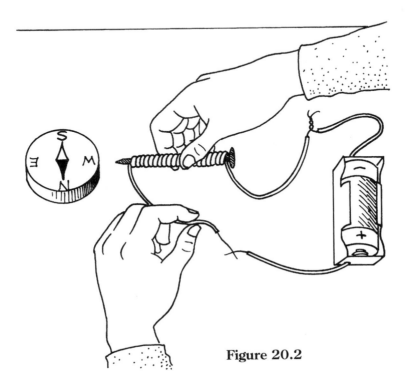

Figure 20.2

the ends of the wire. Allow the compass to align with Earth's magnetic north. With a 1.5-volt battery in a battery holder, twist together the bare end of one solenoid wire and the bare end of one battery-holder wire. Hold the electromagnet so that the pointed end of the nail is near but not touching the west side of the compass. While in this position, touch the free solenoid wire and the free battery wire together for about 1 second. Note the direction in which the north end of the compass needle moves. If the end of the nail pointing toward the compass attracts the north end of the compass needle, the end is the south pole of the electromagnet. If the north end of the needle is repelled, the nail's end is the north pole of the electromagnet. Reverse the direction of the battery and repeat the procedure.

4. How does the number of wire coils in an electromagnet affect the strength of the magnetic field? Design an experiment to test the magnetic strength of an electromagnet. One way is to use the electromagnet from the previous experiment made of 3 feet (90 cm) of insulated wire. Assemble a circuit using the electromagnet, a 1.5-volt D battery in a battery holder, and a switch. Tape the electromagnet to the edge of a wooden table as shown in Figure 20.3. Use metal paper clips to

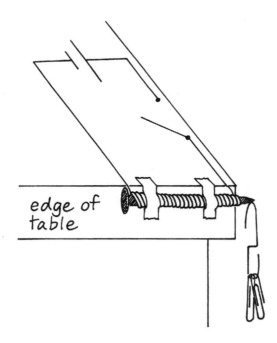

Figure 20.3

test the strength of the electromagnet. Bend one paper clip to form a hook that other paper clips can be hung on. Close the switch and touch the paper clip hook to the pointed end of the nail. Add paper clips to the hook one at a time until the weight of the clips causes the hook to pull away from the nail. Then repeat the experiment using twice as much wire—6 feet (180 cm)—to make the electromagnet. If all the coils will not fit on the nail, wind them as tightly as possible, then wind the next layer over the top, still turning in the same direction. **CAUTION:** *If you feel any warmth through the insulated area of the nail, open the switch. Do not touch the bare nail or bare ends of the wire, because electric current flowing through the wire can cause these areas to get hot enough to burn your skin.*

Get the Facts

1. Television images are the result of thousands of electrons hitting the television screen. What effect do electromagnets play in the direction in which the electrons move? For information, see P. Erik Gundersen, *The Handy Physics Answer Book* (Detroit: Visible Ink, 1999), pp. 329–330.

2. *MAGLEV* stands for "magnetically levitated." How are MAGLEV trains different from conventional trains? For information, see P. Erik Gundersen, *The Handy Physics Answer Book* (Detroit: Visible Ink, 1999), pp. 330–331.

3. *Left-hand* rules are used to find force on current or moving particles in a magnetic field. They are also used to find direction of a magnetic field caused by current in straight wires as well as in solenoids. What are the left-hand rules? How do left-hand rules and right-hand rules compare? For information, see physics texts.

PART IV

Heat

21 Thermal Conduction: Transfer of Vibrational Energy

Thermal energy is the sum of all the kinetic and potential energy of the particles in random motion making up an object. The faster the particles are moving, the hotter the substance. The term "heat" is often used very loosely. It is commonly said that hot objects possess more heat than do cold objects, but technically the energy in the hot object is not heat, it is thermal energy. Heat is the movement of thermal energy from one object to another as a result of differences in temperature. The process by which heat is transferred from one particle to another by collisions of the particles is called thermal conduction.

In this project, you will determine the effects of distance, time, cross-sectional area, and types of materials and temperature on thermal conduction. You will also compare the efficiency of different thermal insulators.

Getting Started

Purpose   To determine how distance affects thermal conduction.

Materials

lemon-size piece of modeling clay
one small birthday candle
metal cookie sheet or baking pan
1 small paper clip
permanent marker
metric ruler
margarine
18-by-30-inch (45-by-75-cm) piece of aluminum foil
transparent tape
kitchen matches

141

Procedure

1. Use a grape-size piece of clay to stand the candle in the metal cookie sheet, as shown in Figure 21.1.

2. Unbend the paper clip to form a metal wire that is as straight as possible.

3. Use the marker and the ruler to make marks on the wire at 2 cm, 4 cm, and 6 cm starting from one end.

4. Use the remaining clay to form a cylindrical holder for the wire that is about 3 inches (7.5 cm) tall. You should be able to stick one end of the wire into the side of the clay holder so that when wire is held parallel to the table, the free end of the wire will be above the candle wick (in the top of the flame when the wick is lit, as shown in Figure 21.1).

5. Place balls of margarine about ½ inch (1.25 cm) in diameter on the marks on the wire.

6. Fold the aluminum foil in half, placing the long sides together. Then connect the ends with tape, forming a circle about 4 inches (10 cm) high.

7. Place the circle of aluminum foil around the candle, wire, and clay cylindrical holder. This will shield the materials from drafts.

8. Use a match to light the candle.

9. With the end of the wire in the tip of the flame, observe the samples of margarine. Make note of the order in which the samples show any sign of melting. When all of the samples show signs of melting, blow out the flame.

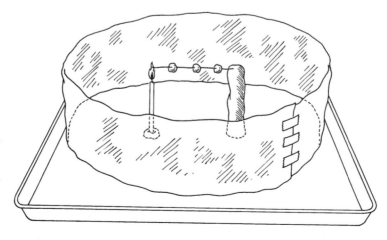

Figure 21.1

Results

The samples of margarine melt in order of placement from the flame with the margarine sample closest to the flame showing the first signs of melting and the farthest sample from the flame melting last.

Why?

Thermal energy or **internal energy** is the sum of the kinetic and potential energy of random motion of particles making up an object. The transfer of thermal energy from one object or region to another due to differences in temperature is called **heat.** Heat moves from a hot object or region to a colder one. **Thermal conduction** or **conduction** is the transfer of heat when energetic particles collide with some of their less energetic neighboring particles. Thus conduction is the movement of heat through a substance from a region of high temperature to a region of lower temperature. Conduction occurs in fluids when their moving molecules collide. But conduction is more commonly the method of heat transfer through a solid material without the movement of the solid material itself. Materials through which heat flows readily are called **thermal conductors** or **conductors.** Metals, such as the paper clip in this experiment, are particularly good conductors of heat because of a high concentration of free electrons (electrons in some solids, particularly metals, that are attracted relatively equally to all nearby atoms and are not tightly bound to a single site and are relatively free to move through the solid), which transfers heat when they collide with the atoms of the metal. The measure of the ability of a material to conduct heat is called **thermal conductivity.**

If a substance is heated, as the wire is in this investigation, the heat is conducted from the heated end to the cooler end. The fact that the margarine sample closest to the heated end of the wire melts first, followed by the second sample and then the third, shows that it takes time for the heat to be conducted from the hotter end of the wire to the cooler end. Thus the amount of heat conducted through the metal wire from the warmer end to the cooler end is proportional to the time during which conduction has been taking place.

Try New Approaches

1. How does the cross-sectional area of a metal affect the heat conducted through it? Repeat the experiment using a paper clip with a larger cross-sectional area. Determine if the amount of heat conducted is proportional to or inversely proportional to the cross-sectional area of a material.

2. How does the type of metal affect heat conduction? Repeat the original experiment using different types of wire with the same cross-sectional area, thus the same **gauge** (a measure of standard size). Wire strippers have gauge sizes that can be used to measure the circumference of wire. Generally a small paper clip is 22-gauge and is made of steel. Use a piece of wire of equal gauge and length but made of different material, such as copper. Be sure to strip away all of the insulation from the wire. Prepare two clay holders and place them on opposite sides of the candle. Position both so they are at the same height and have the same amount of metal in the flame. A larger diameter foil circle will be needed. Compare the time it takes for each margarine sample to melt. For information about thermal conductors, see Mary Jones, *Physics* (New York: Cambridge University Press, 1997), pp. 82–83.

Design Your Own Experiment

1. Does length of a wire affect heat conduction? Design an experiment to show the effect of length on the thermal conductivity of a conductor. One way is to repeat step 2 in "Try New Approaches," using two wires of the same gauge but different lengths. When the first sample of margarine shows signs of melting, blow out the candle. Continue to observe the remaining samples of margarine. Use the results to determine if the same amount of heat is transferred from one end of the wire to the other.

2. How is temperature difference between two materials related to heat conduction between them? Design a way to determine if a larger temperature difference causes more or less heat to flow from one material to another. One way is to fill two Styrofoam cups one-fourth full with water. Put hot tap water in cup A and cold tap water in cup B. Measure the temperatures of the hot and the cold water. Place two or more metal washers in the hot water. After 3 minutes, use a spoon to remove the washers from the hot water and place them in cup B, the cup of cold water. At the end of 1 minute, stir the water in cup B, then measure the temperature of the water in the cup. Note the difference between the original temperature of the cold water and the temperature after the warm washers had been in the water for 1 minute. Repeat twice, first using warm water in cup B made warm by mixing equal amounts of hot and cold tap water. Then use water in cup B made cold by adding one or more ice cubes to the water. (Allow the ice to remain in the water for 2 minutes, stir, then remove the ice before adding the washers.) For more information about a material's **temperature gradient** (the temperature change with distance along a material), see Corine Stockley, *Illustrated Dictionary of Physics* (London: Usborne, 2000), p. 28.

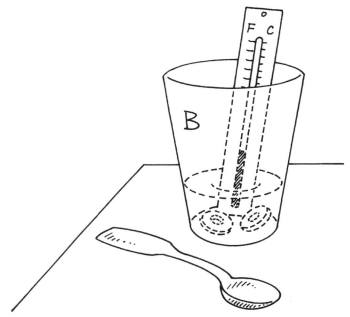

Figure 21.2

3. Insulators are materials with a low concentration of free electrons, and **thermal insulators** are poor conductors of heat. These materials, such as glass, paper, and Styrofoam, depend on the interaction of vibrating atoms and molecules to transfer heat, which is a less efficient method than by movement of free electrons in conductors. Thus less heat is conducted by thermal insulators. Design an experiment to compare the insulating properties of materials used to hold hot liquids. One way is to use cups each made of different insulating materials. Add equal amounts of hot water to each cup. Place a thermometer in each container. Measure the temperature of the water in each container every 2 minutes for 20 minutes or until no further temperature changes occur. Record the temperature in a Temperature/ Insulation Data table like Table 21.1. Use the data to prepare a graph, and record the information for each material on the graph, using a different-color ink for each.

Table 21.1 Temperature/Insulation Data									
Materials	Temperature, °F (°C)								
	Time, minutes								
	2	4	6	8	10	12	14	16	18	20
glass										
paper										
Styrofoam										

Get the Facts

1. *Specific heat* of a substance is the amount of energy that must be added to raise the temperature of a unit mass one temperature unit. When 1 calorie of heat is added to 1 gram of water, the water's temperature rises 1°C. What are the specific heats of other materials, such as aluminum? How can specific heat be used to determine the amount of heat transferred through a metal? For information, see "specific heat" in a physics text.

2. Temperature-sensitive nerve endings in your skin can detect differences between the temperature inside and outside your body. You sense an object as feeling cold when heat is transferred from your body to that object. Why do some things that are the same temperature but made of different materials, such as a carpet and a tile floor, feel as if they have different temperatures? For information, see Annabel Craig, *Science Encyclopedia* (London: Usborne, 1988), p. 14.

22 Convection: Movement of Heat through Fluids

Heat is the movement of energy from an object with high thermal energy to one with lower thermal energy. Convection is the process by which heat is transferred by the bulk movement of a fluid (gas or liquid). Natural convection is the up-and-down movement of fluids due to differences in temperature. Forced convection is when an external device, such as a fan, causes the circulation of warm or cool air.

In this project, you will investigate how water's temperature affects its movement. You will determine how an area can be warmed or cooled by convection currents. You will also find the temperature at various heights in a room and use the results to determine if there are convection currents in that room.

Getting Started

Purpose: To determine how water's temperature affects its movement.

Materials
1-quart (1-liter) jar
cold and hot tap water
4 or 5 ice cubes
spoon
coffee cup
blue food coloring
eyedropper

Procedure
1. Fill the jar about half full with cold water.
2. Add the ice cubes to the jar of water.
3. Use the spoon to stir the ice and water mixture to cool the water; then remove any undissolved ice.
4. Fill the cup about one-fourth full with hot tap water.

147

5. Add 10 or more drops of food coloring to the hot water. Stir.

6. Fill the eyedropper with the hot, colored water.

7. Place the tip of the eyedropper against the inside of the jar about 1 inch (2.5 cm) above the water. As you observe from the side of the jar, slowly squeeze the eyedropper so the water runs down the inside of the jar into the cold water. Make note of the motion of the hot, colored water after it enters the cold water.

8. Repeat step 7 four times.

9. Observe the contents of the jar periodically for 10 minutes or until no more changes are seen.

Figure 22.1

Results

Some of the blue colored water sinks a short distance in the cold water, while some immediately moves across its surface. Most of the colored water that sank very quickly rises and joins the other colored water on and near the surface of the cold water. After a time, the blue water sinks, and all of the water becomes slightly blue in color.

Why?

An object's thermal energy is the sum of all the kinetic and potential energy of all the particles making up the object. Heat is the movement of thermal energy from an object with high thermal energy to one with lower thermal energy. In other words, thermal energy is transferred from a warm object to a cooler one. As a fluid warms by the absorption of heat, its thermal energy increases, and thus the kinetic energy of its particles increases. This causes the particles to **expand** (mover farther apart thus occupying more volume), resulting in a decrease in density. So the hot, colored water is less dense than the cold water in the jar. When poured into the jar, the hot, colored water's **momentum** (value describing the amount of motion an object has) carries it below the surface of the cold water. But then the bulk of the hot, colored water rises above the cold water because the hot water is less dense. The greater the difference in the temperature of the water, the greater the difference in their densities.

As the hot, colored water cools, it descends, and eventually all of the water mixes. When all of the water is the same temperature, the colored water no longer moves up or down but rather spreads out by **diffusion** (the movement of fluids due to molecular motion). The rising and descending of a fluid due to differences between its density and the density of a surrounding fluid produces what is called a **convection current.** **Convection** is the process by which heat is transferred from place to place by the movement of a fluid. **Natural convection** is the movement of fluids due to difference in temperature. Differences in temperature cause the density at one place in a fluid to be different from that at another. **Forced convection** is the use of an external device, such as a fan, to cause the transfer of heat from place to place by the movement of a fluid.

Try New Approaches

1a. How would reversing the two temperatures affect the results? Repeat the investigation, filling the jar with hot water and the eyedropper with cold water. How does this model an atmospheric condition called an inversion? For more information on convection currents, see *Janice VanCleave's A+ Projects in Earth Science* (New York: Wiley, 1999), pp. 175–179.

b. The looping path that a convection current follows is called a **convection cell.** Use a diagram to show the motion of a fluid in a convection cell. For information, see Corinne Stockley, *Illustrated Dictionary of Physics* (London: Usborne, 2000), p. 28.

Design Your Own Experiment

1a. Convection currents are used to cool an area, such as in a refrigerator. Design a way to show how the location of the cooling coils in the top of a refrigerator creates a cooling convection current. One way is to use the motion of water at different temperatures. Do this by filling a paper cup with cold water and adding 2 drops of food coloring to the water. Stir. Cover the mouth of the cup with a small square of aluminum foil. Insert a ⅛-by-10-inch (0.3-by-25-cm) dowel through the center of the aluminum foil. The dowel should stand as vertically as possible. Place the cup in a freezer. When the water is frozen, remove the paper cup from the freezer, then remove the paper and the aluminum foil from the ice. The dowel should be firmly frozen in the ice. Fill a jar that has a mouth large enough for the ice to fit through about three-fourths full with hot tap water. Push the ice just below the surface of the water in the jar and secure it in this position by taping the dowel to the rim of the bottle. (See Figure 22.2.) Observe the contents of the bottle for 1 to 2 minutes. Notice the direction of any convection currents.

b. If cooling coils were placed at the bottom of a refrigerator, what effect would this have on the creation of cooling convention currents?

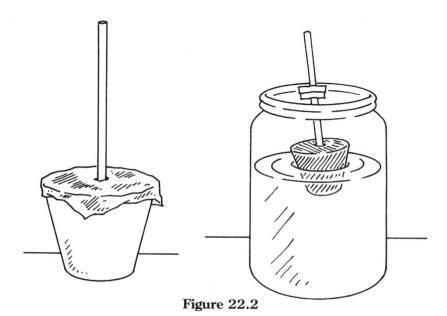

Figure 22.2

2. It is commonly said that "heat rises," but what is meant is that the lighter, less dense hot fluids rise through cooler, denser fluids. Design a way to show that warm air rises and cool air sinks. One way is to secure three thermometers to a wall. Lay three thermometers on a table for 3 or more minutes so they all register the same temperature, then put one thermometer near the floor, a second on the middle of the wall, and a third near the ceiling. If there is a ceiling fan, turn it off during the investigation. Record the initial temperature readings of the three thermometers in a Temperature Data table like Table 22.1. Then record the temperature readings on each thermometer every 15 minutes for 1 hour. Determine the absolute differences between the temperatures at the different heights. For example, if T_1 is 75°F and T_2 is 78°F, the absolute difference between T_1 and T_2 expressed as $|T_1 - T_2|$ is the positive difference between these two values, which is 3°F (78°F – 75°F).

From your results, determine if there are convection currents in the room. If so, what is the direction of the currents?

Table 22.1 Temperature Data						
Time/min	Thermometers					
	T_1 (floor)	T_2 (middle)	Absolute T_3 (ceiling)	Absolute Difference $|T_1-T_2|$	Absolute Difference $|T_2-T_3|$	Difference $|T_1-T_3|$
0						
15						
30						
45						
60						
average						

Get The Facts

When Earth's surface is heated by solar energy, it warms the air above it, creating convection currents. The currents of rising, heated air are called *updrafts* or *thermals*. How do thermals affect air pollution? How do thermals affect the weather? For information, see Curt Suplee, *Everyday Science Explained* (Washington, D.C.: National Geographic Society, 1998), pp. 70–71.

23 Infrared Radiation: Heat Transferred through Space

Electromagnetic radiation is energy transferred by electromagnetic waves (waves consisting of oscillating electric and magnetic fields moving at the speed of light). Solar energy is electromagnetic radiation. All of the electromagnetic waves making up electromagnetic radiation are called the electromagnetic spectrum; infrared radiation and visible light are part of this spectrum.

In this project, you will determine the effect of color on the absorption and emission of infrared radiation in solar energy. You will discover how the surface area of an object affects how much infrared radiation it will absorb. You will also compare infrared radiation from space to infrared radiation from Earth's surface.

Getting Started

Purpose: To determine the effect of color on the absorption of infrared radiation.

Materials

two 4-by-4-inch (10-by-10-cm) squares of construction paper, 1 black, 1 white
2 thermometers
transparent tape
scissors
6-by-12-inch (15-by-30-cm) piece of heavy cardboard or a board of comparable size (size is not critical)
walnut-size piece of clay
pencil
watch

Procedure

1. Make a paper cover for one of the thermometers by wrapping a single layer of the black paper around the thermometer's bulb, folding the bottom edge over the end of the thermometer. Secure the paper with tape. You have a prepared a black paper–thermometer system.

2. Repeat step 1, using the white paper and the second thermometer. You have prepared a white paper–thermometer system.

3. Record the thermometer reading on each thermometer as the starting temperatures in a Paper–Thermometer Systems Data table like Table 23.1.

4. Lay the paper–thermometer systems side by side on the cardboard and secure them with tape.

5. Use the clay to stand the pencil vertically at one end of the cardboard.

6. Take the cardboard outside on a sunny day and place it on the ground. The surface of each packet on the cardboard should be at a 90° angle to the Sun's rays. To obtain this angle, use dirt to elevate the end of the cardboard where the pencil stands so that the pencil casts no shadow, or the shadow is only a small area around the base of the pencil. Adjust the cardboard periodically during the experiment to keep its surface at or near a 90° angle to the Sun's rays.

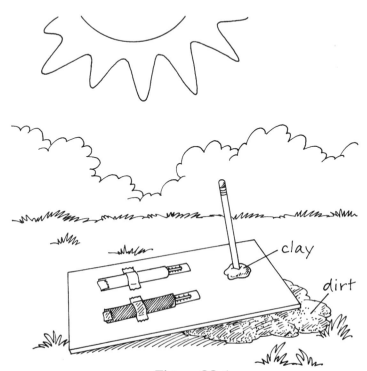

Figure 23.1

7. Every minute for a total of 5 minutes, read the temperature on each thermometer and record it in the table. Then, every 10 minutes for 60 minutes, read the temperature on each thermometer and record it in the data table.

Table 23.1 Paper–Thermometer Systems Data		
Time (min)	Temperature, °F (°C) Black Paper–Thermometer System	Temperature, °F (°C) White Paper–Thermometer System
Starting, 0		
1		
2		
3		
4		
5		
15		
25		
35		
45		
55		
65		

Results

The temperature of the black paper–thermometer system changes faster. In time, the temperatures of both systems stop changing, with the black one at a higher temperature.

Why?

A **wave** is a periodic disturbance in a **medium** (substance through which something acts) or **space** (region without a medium). Waves transfer energy from one place to another. **Electromagnetic radiation** is energy transferred by electromagnetic waves; it can travel through space. **Electromagnetic waves** are transverse waves moving at the speed of light and consisting of rapidly alternating electric and magnetic fields at right angles to each other and to the direction in which the waves are traveling. (**Transverse waves** look like water waves in which

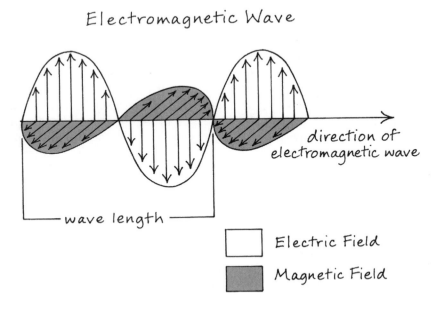

Figure 23.2

the vibrations are perpendicular to the direction in which the waves are traveling.) The **wavelength** (distance between corresponding points of two successive waves) is shown in Figure 23.2. Electromagnetic radiation is also called **radiant energy.** The range of wavelengths over which electromagnetic radiation extends is called the **electromagnetic spectrum.** The electromagnetic spectrum, in order from short to long waves, consists of gamma rays, X rays, ultraviolet radiation, visible light, infrared radiation, microwaves, and radio waves.

Solar energy is electromagnetic radiation from the Sun containing the entire electromagnetic spectrum, including large amounts of **infrared radiation** (electromagnetic radiation whose wavelengths lie just beyond the red portion of visible light; also called heat waves). When infrared radiation is absorbed by an object, the object becomes hotter because its thermal energy increases. Absorption of infrared radiation by surface molecules accelerates their motion. As the movement of molecules in a material increases, the thermal energy and therefore the temperature of the material increase.

In this investigation, infrared radiation is absorbed by the paper—thermometer systems. This is evident by their increase in temperature. The only difference between the two systems is the color of the paper. The temperature of the black system rose at a much faster rate than that of the white system, indicating that the black paper was absorbing more infrared radiation than the white paper. When the systems became hotter than the surrounding air, they lost heat (transfer of thermal energy from one object to another) by conduction, convection, and **radiation** (the process by which hot bodies lose heat in the form of infrared radiation). In time the temperature of each system reached a **thermal equilibrium,** the state of a system in which the gain and loss of energy are equal. The temperature of the black system at thermal equilibrium is higher than that of the white system at thermal equilibrium because the black system has absorbed more infrared radiation from the light. Thus the black system has a high rate of energy inflow.

Try New Approaches

1. How does the surface area of a material affect the amount of radiation that it absorbs? Repeat the investigation, turning the paper packets so that their narrow edges are facing the Sun.

2. Does the color of the systems affect the rate at which they emit radiation? Design a way to cool the systems. One way would be to place each system in a plastic, resealable bag and lay the bags in an ice chest.

Design Your Own Experiment

1a. How does the heat radiating from space compare with that radiating from Earth's surface? Design a way to measure radiation from a specific direction. One way is to make a heat telescope to capture the radiation. A heat telescope could be made by placing a thermometer inside an aluminum foil cone. Two heat telescopes, one pointed at the sky and the other toward Earth, could be used to compare the radiation from the two directions. Each telescope could be made using a 12-by-18-inch (30-by-45-cm) piece of heavy-duty aluminum foil. Place the shorter sides of the foil piece together and fold over the ends several times to form a cylinder. Insert the bulb end of the thermometer into the narrow end of the aluminum foil cylinder. Squeeze the foil around the thermometer, forming a funnel shape. Adjust the position of the thermometer so that the bulb is just above the bottom of the foil cylinder. Allow the two heat telescopes to remain side by side on a table for 2 or more minutes until they register the same temperature. Record this temperature as the initial temperature, T_1, for both thermometers. On a clear day, take the two heat telescopes outdoors. At the same time, point one heat telescope toward the sky and the other toward the ground. After 1 or more minutes, read and record the temperature readings of each heat telescope, as the final temperature, T_f. Repeat the experiment four or more times. Calculate the change in temperature due to radiation from space (ΔT_s) by determining the absolute difference between T_i and T_f for the heat telescope pointed toward the sky. Calculate the change in temperature due to the radiation from Earth's surface (ΔT_e) by determining the absolute difference between T_i and T_f for the heat telescope pointed toward the ground. Average the results for each telescope.

b. Calculate a space-to-Earth radiation ratio using this equation:

$$\Delta T_s / \Delta T_E$$

Is the space/Earth radiation ratio the same at night? Repeat the previous investigation at night.

c. What effect, if any, do barriers such as trees have on radiation from space? Is there more radiation coming from one direction of the sky than from another? Do different surfaces on Earth affect how much radiation comes from Earth? Design ways to answer these questions using the heat telescope.

Get the Facts

1. An object's ability to absorb and emit radiation is called its *emissivity.* A perfect blackbody or, simply, a blackbody has an emissivity of 1. What is a blackbody, and how does its emissivity compare to that of other objects? For information, see Louis A. Bloomfield, *How Things Work: The Physics of Everyday Life* (New York: Wiley, 1997), p. 268.

2. Solar radiation consists mainly of visible light, ultraviolet radiation, and infrared radiation. How do these forms of radiation differ? For information, see Mary and Geoff Jones, *Physics* (New York: Cambridge University Press, 1997), pp. 116–117.

PART V

Light

24 Polarization: Vibrations in One Direction

Unpolarized light consists of waves with electric fields vibrating in all directions. In some cases, however, all the waves in a beam vibrate in one direction or in one plane. Such light is said to be polarized.

In this project, you will investigate polarized and unpolarized light. You will determine what an analyzer does to polarized light. You will determine if the angle of incidence (angle that light strikes a surface) affects the degree of horizontal polarization. You will also test the optical activity of different solid materials and of different concentrations of water solutions.

Getting Started

Purpose: To polarize light.

Materials
desk lamp with incandescent bulb
inexpensive, plastic polarized sunglasses

Procedure
1. Turn on the lamp and position it so that the bulb is visible. Stand at a distance of about 3 feet (1 m) from the bulb. Look at the bulb and make note of its brightness.

2. Remove the lenses from the sunglasses by twisting the frames and popping the plastic lenses out.

3. At a distance of about 3 feet (1 m), close one eye and look through one of the polarized lenses at the lit bulb and again note the bulb's brightness. This will be called lens A.

4. Hold the second lens (called lens B) in front of but not touching lens A and, while still closing one eye, look at the light through both lenses. Hold lens A in place while rotating lens B until the bulb

161

Figure 24.1

appears at its brightest when viewed through both lenses. Then slowly rotate lens B 90°, observing any change in the brightness of the bulb.

Results

The bulb is less bright when viewed through one lens. Viewing the bulb through two lenses further decreases its brightness. As one of the lenses is rotated in front of the other lens, the light decreases still further until it is no longer visible or only partly visible.

Why?

Visible light is a form of radiation, which is energy that travels in the form of electromagnetic waves. Light is made of transverse waves that vibrate in all directions perpendicular to the direction of the motion of the light. **Polarized light** is light in which the electric fields of the light waves vibrate in a direction parallel to each other. **Polarization** of light refers to the direction of the electric field in an electromagnetic wave of light. A light wave whose electric field is vibrating in the vertical direction is said to be **vertically polarized.** A light wave whose electric field is vibrating in the horizontal direction is said to be **horizontally polar-ized. Unpolarized light** contains light waves with electric fields vibrat-ing in different directions, such as the light from the bulb in this experiment. (See Figure 24.2.) A polarized lens acts as a **polarizer,** which is a material that allows electric fields of light vibrating in only one direction or one plane to pass through it. When unpolarized light strikes a polarized lens, part of the light is **reflected** (bounced off of), part is absorbed by the lens, and the part with electric fields vibrating in one specific plane passes through. The light emerges from the other side of the polarizer as polarized light. Figure 24.2 represents vertical polariza-tion. Polarized sunglasses are generally made of plastic material in which needlelike crystals are embedded. These crystals line up parallel to one another and make a polarized lens act as though it consists of many slitlike openings parallel to one another, so only those light waves with electric fields vibrating in the same plane as the parallel slits in the polarizer get through.

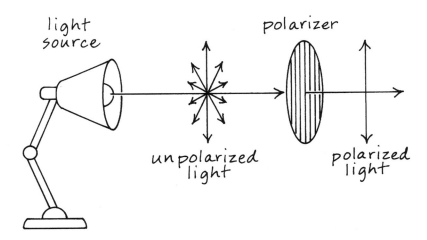

Figure 24.2

Placing the two polarized lenses together demonstrates the effect of using two polarizers aligned with one another. The first lens in line with the light is called the polarizer, and the second lens is called the **analyzer** (a polarizer used to determine if light is polarized). When the crystals in the two lenses are lined up parallel to one another, the greatest amount of light possible passes through. In this position, rotat-ing the analyzer 90° results in the crystals in the separate lenses being at right angles to one another. None of the polarized light is able to pass through the analyzer in this position, as shown in Figure 24.3. **Science Fair Hint:** Use diagrams such as the ones shown to represent the results of this investigation.

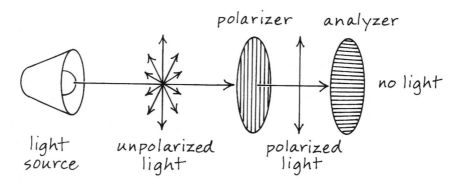

Figure 24.3

Try New Approaches

How is light affected by nonpolarized lenses? Repeat the experiment, using the lenses from an inexpensive pair of nonpolarized sunglasses.

Design Your Own Experiment

1a. Unpolarized light becomes partially polarized when reflected from nonmetallic surfaces, such as water or glass, while some is transmitted and/or absorbed. The parallel components of the **incident light** (light striking a surface) are largely reflected. The reflected light is partially polarized in a direction parallel with the surface it reflects from. Thus for lakes and other surfaces parallel to Earth's surface, the reflected light is said to be horizontally polarized. There is a special **angle of incidence** (angle between incident light and a line perpendicular to the surface it strikes) called the **polarization angle** at which the reflected light from a nonmetallic surface is completely polarized. Design a way to determine the approximate magnitude of the polarization angle for light reflecting from water. One way is to fill a large bowl with water and set it on a table. In a darkened room, hold a flashlight above the water so that its light is perpendicular (normal or 90°) to the water's surface, then slightly tilt the flashlight. Sit facing the bowl and view the water's surface through a polarized lens. Since the water acts as a polarizer, the lens acts as an analyzer. Part of the light will enter the water and form a light spot on the bottom of the bowl and part will reflect, thus forming an **image** (a representation of a physical object formed by light reflected from a surface) of the end of the flashlight. Rotate the analyzer to determine if the reflected light from the water's surface is polarized. The degree of polarization will be determined by how much of the reflected light (the image) disappears. If you see no change in the image, it indicates that the reflected light is not polarized. If all of the image disappears, then the reflected light is 100% polarized. Increase the angle of incidence by tilting the flashlight more and analyze the reflection at the new angle. Continue this until the flashlight is held parallel to the water's surface. Estimate the angle of the flashlight from perpendicular (the incidence angle) and devise a way to compare the degree of polarization for each angle, such as a rating of 0 to +5, with +5 being the greatest polarization. For information about polarized angles, see Craig F. Bohren, *What Light through Yonder Window Breaks?* (New York: Wiley, 1991), pp. 37–40. For information about horizontal and vertical polarization, see Louis A. Bloomfield, *How Things Work* (New York: Wiley, 1997), pp. 494, 498, and 529–530.

b. How does the material of the reflective surface affect polarization? Repeat the previous investigation, using different materials, including a smooth metal such as a flat baking pan. For information about polarization from reflected surfaces, see Karl F. Kuhn, *Basic Physics* (New York: Wiley, 1996), pp. 79–80.

2a. A material is said to be **optically active** when it rotates the plane of the light waves passing through it. Design a way to test the optical activity of materials, such as by placing a material between two polarized lenses. For example, to test the optical activity of a plastic cup, place the lamp, polarizer, cup, and analyzer in a straight line with one another. Rotate the analyzer and observe the changing patterns of colors. To test the optical activity of transparent tape, you can stretch some of the tape across a small open frame cut from poster board. Place the lamp, polarizer, tape, and analyzer in line with one another. Rotate the analyzer and observe the color patterns. For more information about the colors seen in optically active materials when viewed through an analyzer, see Hazel Rossoti, *Colour: Why the World Isn't Grey* (Princeton, N.J.: Princeton University Press, 1983), pp. 49–51.

b. Sugar and tartaric acid (cream of tartar) are known to be optically active. Design a method of testing different concentrations of solutions of water and these chemicals. Note that the container used to hold the solutions must not be optically active. Test light passing through empty containers for optical activity and select one that is optically inactive. Devise a method of comparing the degree of optical activity of each concentration.

Get the Facts

When two polarized lenses are placed together, the amount of light passing through the analyzer is greatest when their crystals are parallel and least when they are perpendicular such that no light gets through. Since the light exiting the polarizer is polarized, why does any of it pass through the lenses when the crystals in one lens are positioned between 0° and 90° relative to the crystals in the second lens? What are photons, and how does their spin affect polarization? For information, see John Gribbin, *In Search of Schrödinger's Cat* (New York: Bantam, 1984), pp. 218–229.

Scattering: Receiving and Transmitting Light

25

Particles in materials act as tiny antennas (devices that send and/or receive electromagnetic radiation) by receiving visible light, which is made up of electromagnetic waves, and transmitting the waves in new directions. This process is called Raleigh scattering, after English physicist Lord Raleigh (John William Strutt, 1842–1919). In 1871, he solved the question of why the sky looks blue by describing how light is scattered.

In this project, you will determine the effect of small particles on the scattering of light. You will investigate how particle size affects the scattering angle of light. You will also discover how the scattering angle affects the brightness of a substance.

Getting Started

Purpose: To demonstrate the effect of small particles on the scattering of light.

Materials

1 sheet of white copy paper
flashlight
two 10-ounce (300-ml) colorless, transparent, plastic cups
distilled water
permanent marker
eyedropper
whole milk
spoon
6-by-12-inch (15-by-30-cm) piece of white poster board

Procedure

1. Lay the sheet of paper on a table and lay the flashlight so that its bulb end is in the center of one of the longer edges of the paper.

167

2. Fill the cups with water.

3. With the marker, label the cups A and B.

4. Add one drop of milk to cup B and stir.

5. Bend the poster board in half by placing the short ends together to form a stand-up screen. Set the screen at the edge of the paper opposite the flashlight.

6. With the flashlight on, darken the room and note the color of the light from the flashlight on the paper screen.

7. Set cup A in the center of the paper in front of the flashlight and do the following:

   ■ Note the color of the light on the screen after it has passed through the water.

   ■ Looking down on the water, note any change in the color of the water.

8. Repeat step 7, using cup B.

Figure 25.1

Results

The color of the flashlight's beam when it is seen on the screen after traveling through the air can vary from white to yellowish. When the flashlight beam passes through plain water, you don't notice a change in the color of the light on the screen or the color of the water. But milky water makes the light on the screen appear more yellow to orange and the milky water appears bluish.

Why?

Light, like other electromagnetic radiation, shows both wave and particle properties. Its propagation (motion) is wavelike, but its interaction with matter occurs as if the radiation travels as particles consisting of the unit of energy associated with each frequency of radiation, called a **quantum.** The particles are called **photons** (packets of energy consisting of a quantum of electromagnetic radiation that has both a particle and wave behavior). Since photons oscillate like a wave, the size of a photon is considered to be equal to the light's wavelength when acting as a wave.

The flashlight is a source of white light, which is visible light (the part of the electromagnetic spectrum to which the eye is sensitive) made of all colors of light—all wavelengths from red, the longest, to blue and violet, the shortest. When all the wavelengths of light are mixed together, your eye receives them and your brain interprets the combination as white light—no color. Without milk in the water, light travels through the water without being seen as a color. But with the milk, the water has a bluish color and the light transmitted to the screen has a yellowish to orange color. This change is due to **scattering** (the deflection or spreading out of a beam of electromagnetic radiation as it passes through material) of some of the light waves. Scattering can be a combination of processes, one being **elastic scattering** (reflection—bouncing off of), in which photons collide with and bounce off particles, much like the collision of two billiard balls and their bouncing off each other. A photon is scattered best when it collides with a particle approximately its own size. The short wavelengths—violet and blue—are scattered most by the small milk particles in the water. Thus as the white light passes through the milky water, a mixture of wavelengths that give the overall sensation of a pale blue color are scattered. Violet—the shortest wavelength—would be in that mix, as would some of the longer wavelengths as well. As the incident light (light that strikes the surface of a material) hits the milk particles, the mixture of short wavelengths is scattered from the light, and the remaining parts of the light transmitted to the screen have a yellow to orange color (see Figure 25.2). Note that if the particle is bigger than the largest wavelength in visible light, then the scattered light contains all of the wavelengths; thus the light is white.

Try New Approaches

How does the concentration of particles affect scattering? Repeat the investigation, this time comparing cups of water with 0 to 10 drops of milk in them. Record the color of the water and the transmitted light for each concentration in a Scattering Data table like Table 25.1.

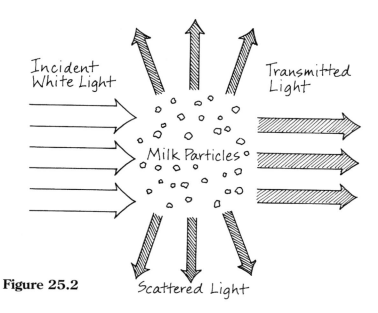

Figure 25.2

Table 25.1 Scattering Data		
Milk Concentration, Drops of Milk per 1 Cup of Water	Color of Water	Color of Transmitted Light
0		
1		
2		
3		
4		
5		
6		
7		
8		
9		
10		

Design Your Own Experiment

The speed of light varies with the density of the material it passes through. The greater the density, the slower the speed. Design a way to demonstrate that the greater the change in the speed of light when it hits a particle, the greater the light is scattered. One way to compare scattering is to compare the brightness of a material. Since the speed of light in air is about 3×10^8 m/s and 2.23×10^8 m/s in water, compare the brightness of wet and dry sand. Note that incident light to the dry sand passes through air, and the incident light to the wet sand passes through water. Fill a paper plate with sand. Add water to one part of the sand. From the brightness of each area, determine which has the greater and which has less scattering: dry sand (sand particles surrounded by air), or wet sand (sand particles surrounded by water). You may want to test other liquids, such as cooking oil. For more information about the scattering by wet objects, see Hazel Rossotti, *Colour: Why the World Isn't Grey* (Princeton, N.J.: Princeton University Press, 1983), p. 78.

Get the Facts

Depending on circumstances, scattering can be any combination of three processes as electromagnetic radiation interacts with matter particles. These processes include elastic scattering (reflection), *inelastic scattering* (absorption followed by reradiation), and diffraction (bending of light around an object in its path). What is Rayleigh scattering? For information about scattering, see Robert L. Wolke, *What Einstein Told His Barber* (New York: Dell, 2000), pp. 170–175. For information about Rayleigh scattering, see Jearl Walker, *The Flying Circus of Physics with Answers* (New York: Wiley, 1977).

26 Thin-Film Interference: Light Waves In and Out of Step

Written references to colors being seen in thin films of materials, such as oil on water, have been found on clay tablets dating back several thousand years. Some ancient cultures used the colored patterns produced by oil on water for fortune-telling, but scientists, including Sir Isaac Newton, devised experiments to explain the production of the colors.

In this project, you will observe colors produced by thin films and discover what effect different materials used for the film and the motion of the film have on the colors produced. You will also investigate interference colors in a film of soap bubbles and how the colors are affected by the thickness of the film, the angle of the incident light, and the type of light source.

Getting Started

Purpose: To observe colors in a thin film.

Materials

opaque cereal bowl (**opaque**—not capable of being seen through)
tap water
desk lamp with incandescent bulb
colorless nail polish

Procedure

1. Fill the bowl about three-fourths full with water.

2. Set the bowl near but not directly under a desk lamp.

3. Let one drop of colorless nail polish fall on the water's surface in the bowl.

4. Turn the desk lamp so that its bulb is about 6 inches (15 cm) above the table and is pointing down.

5. Stand so that you can see the surface of the water in the bowl from above as you slowly move the bowl toward the lamp until the bowl is

172

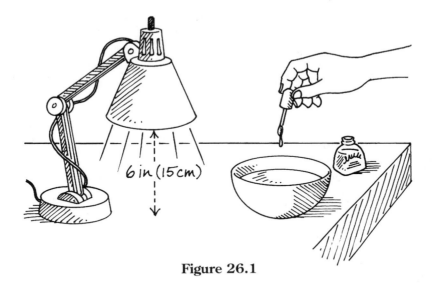

Figure 26.1

beneath it. Make note of any color changes in the nail polish on the water's surface.

Results

Thin bands of colors are seen in the nail polish in the bowl.

Why?

The drop of nail polish spreads out, forming a very thin **transparent** (so clear that it allows light to pass straight through) film on the water's surface in the bowl. White light, such as that from the incandescent bulb of the desk lamp, contains all the visible colored light waves. When white light hits the thin, transparent film, some of the light reflected from the outer surface of the film (wave 1) and some of it entered the film and was reflected from the inner surface (wave 2) (see Figure 26.2). Even though the difference in distance was small, the light reflected from the inner surface traveled a slightly longer distance than the light reflected from the upper surface.

Both reflected waves 1 and 2 are white light with less intensity than the incident light. When the two reflected waves come back together, **superposition** (placing one thing on top of the other) occurs. The separate reflected waves undergo superposition if they are focused by a lens. This occurs in the eye when the eye's lens focuses the light onto the retina. The superposition of one wave on another is called **interference.**

Constructive interference occurs for wavelengths in the reflected waves that are **in phase** (in step). **Constructive interference** is the superposition of two or more waves in phase, resulting in a combined wave with an amplitude larger than the component waves (see Figure 26.3). For example, if constructive interference occurs for the waves of red light in the two reflected waves, the part of the film reflecting these waves has a red color because the red light wave in this area has a much great amplitude and thus is more intense than the other colors of light. Reflected light waves from other parts of the film might have constructive interference for the green light waves; thus this region of the film would appear green, and so on for regions of the film and other colors in the white incident light.

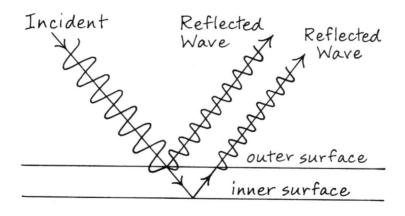

Figure 26.2

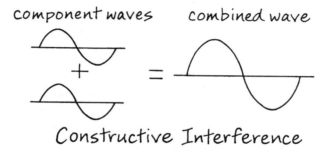

Figure 26.3

Try New Approaches

1. How does the thickness of the film affect the results? Repeat the experiment using a small container of water, such as a bottle cap. For information about interference in thick films, see Craig F. Bohren, *What Light through Yonder Window Breaks?* (New York: Wiley, 1991), pp. 18–19.

2. Does the material that the thin film is made of affect the results? Repeat the experiment using different oils, such as cooking oil, baby oil, and motor oil.

3. How does motion of the material affect the results? Use a toothpick to gently move the material around on the surface of the water as you observe the light reflecting from it.

Design Your Own Experiment

1a. A soap bubble is a combination of soap and water linked together to form a thin layer of elastic liquid surrounding air. Investigate interference colors in the film of soap bubbles. Prepare a bubble solution by combining ¼ cup (63 ml) of dishwashing liquid and 1 cup (250 ml) of tap water in a small bowl. Gently stir. Dip one end of a drinking straw into the bubble solution and blow through the straw. **CAUTION:** *Take care to blow out and not suck in the soapy liquid.* Set the bowl of bubbles near an incandescent light and observe the appearance of the bubbles.

b. Does the angle of the light striking the film affect the results? Design a way to control the angle of the incident light, such as placing the bowl in a box with one hole for light to enter and another hole for viewing.

2a. What effect does the thickness of a soap bubble have on the color produced by interference? Design a way to change the thickness of the soap film. One way is to use gravity. Dip a wire loop into the bubble solution. Holding the loop vertically in front of a dark background, such as a sheet of black paper, watch for colors to appear in the film. Note the difference in colors and patterns at the top and the bottom of the film in the loop. Also, note the color of the film just before it breaks.

b. Another way to measure the angle of the light is to change the angle of the wire loop in relation to a stationary light. Design a way to measure this angle. Photographs of the film could be used to represent the procedure and the results.

Figure 26.4

c. Does the light source affect interference? Repeat the experiment using different light sources, such as fluorescent light and sunlight. For information about the effect of light sources, see Craig F. Bohren, *What Light through Yonder Window Breaks?* (New York: Wiley, 1991), pp. 21–22.

Get the Facts

1. Constructive and destructive interference depend on the thickness of the film. What is destructive interference? What thickness satisfies the requirement for constructive and destructive interference of a specific wavelength? For information on the thickness that produces constructive interference, see Robert L. Lehrman, *Physics the Easy Way* (Hauppauge, N.Y.: Barron's, 1998), pp. 413–414.

2. British scientist Sir Isaac Newton (1642–1727) proposed the corpuscular theory of light. Later, another British scientist, Thomas Young (1773–1829), proposed the wave theory to explain light. How do these two theories differ? Which is used today? Which is used to explain the colors in a thin film? For information, see Tony Rothman, *Instant Physics* (New York: Fawcett Columbine, 1995), pp. 102–107.

27 Convex Lens: Converging Light Rays

A lens is a transparent object that has either two curved surfaces or one plane (flat) surface and one curved surface. Lenses can be made of any transparent material. A lens that has an outward curved surface is called a convex lens. This lens can also be called a converging lens, because it refracts (bends) the light rays passing through it to a central point called the focal point. The distance from the lens to the focal point is called the focal length.

In this project, you will measure the focal length of a convex lens. You will investigate how the diameter and convexity (measure of the outward curve of a surface) of a lens affect its focal length. You will also determine how the position of an object in relation to the focal point of a lens affects image production.

Getting Started

Purpose: To measure the focal length of a convex lens.

Materials
white index card
yardstick (meterstick)
transparent tape
magnifying lens with a 1.5-inch (3.75-cm) or larger diameter

Procedure
1. Lay about ½ inch (1.25 cm) of one short end of the index card on the zero end of the yardstick (meterstick). Tape the card to the stick, and fold the card so that it stands upright, perpendicular to and even with the end of the stick as shown in Figure 27.1. The card is a screen.
2. Stand outdoors in a sunny area with the Sun behind you.
3. Place the free end of the measuring stick on your right shoulder, and support the stick with your left hand.
4. Hold the magnifying lens just above the measuring stick. Move the lens toward the paper screen until a bright light spot forms on the

177

screen. Then move the lens back and forth until a position is found where the spot is as small and as bright as possible. **CAUTION:** *Do not look directly at the Sun, because it can damage your eyes. ALSO: Do not hold the lens in this position for more than 3 to 4 seconds because it can set the card on fire.*

5. Record the distance the lens is from the screen.

Figure 27.1

Results

Light passing through a lens forms a small, bright light spot on a screen.

Why?

A **lens** is a curved transparent material that **refracts** (bends) light, which means it changes the direction of light passing through it. **Convex** means an outward curve. The lens in a magnifying lens is convex on both sides. This is called a **double convex lens** or a double converging lens. A convex lens is thickest in the middle and becomes thinner at the edges. A line through the center of a lens and perpendicular to its surface is called the **principal axis.** All light rays that enter the convex lens parallel to the principal axis are refracted toward the principal axis when they enter the lens as well as when they leave the lens so that they **converge** (come together) at a point called the **focal point** of the lens.

Figure 27.2 is an example of a ray diagram showing light rays coming from a distant source, such as the Sun. These light rays are basically parallel with each other when they reach Earth. When the Sun's rays enter the lens parallel to its principal axis, the lens causes the rays to refract and converge to form a bright spot of light at the focal point of the lens. The distance from the focal point (the spot on the card) to the lens is called the **focal length (F).**

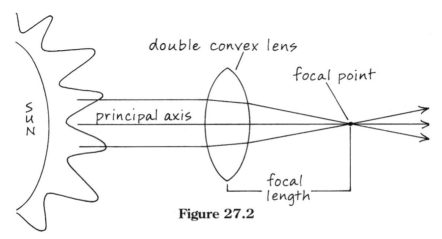

double convex lens

focal point

SUN

principal axis

focal length

Figure 27.2

Try New Approaches

Does the diameter size of a lens affect its focal length (F)? Repeat the investigation using magnifying lenses with different diameters.

Design Your Own Experiment

1. Is there a relationship between focal length (F) and magnification? Design a way to compare the magnification of lenses with different focal lengths. One way is to lay a magnifying lens on the print on this page, then slowly raise it to 1 inch (2.5 cm) above the print. Repeat, using other lenses with different focal lengths. Compare their magnifications.

2. Is it the difference in diameter or the difference in **convexity** (measure of the outward curve of a surface) or roundness that affects the focal length (F) of a lens? Design a way to change the convexity of a

lens without changing its diameter. One way to get approximate comparisons is to make a water-filled lens. Do this by wrapping a 6-inch (15-cm) piece of 20-gauge wire around a pencil to make a round loop. Place a desk lamp on the edge of a desk or tall cabinet so that its light shines down on the floor. Place a white index card on the floor beneath the light. Dip the wire into a bowl of water, with the open loop pointing up. Lift the loop carefully out of the water and hold it just above the index card. You want a large, rounded drop of water to stay in the hole of the wire loop. You have made a thin, water-filled convex lens. Carefully move the water lens away from the card until a position is found where the light spot on the card is brightest. Ask a helper to measure the distance from the wire loop to the card in millimeters. Then, using an eyedropper, carefully add

Figure 27.3

water to the water lens, making it thicker, thus increasing its convexity. Again measure the distance from the card for the water lens to make the brightest spot. Repeat the experiment using water lenses that are thick and thin. Note that while you can compare thick and thin lenses, each repeat may not be the same.

3a. A lens can be used to form an image (a representation of a physical object formed by a lens or a mirror). A **real image** is an image formed by a lens that can be projected on a screen. How does the location of the object affect the position (erect or inverted), location (distance from the lens), and size of the image? Design a way to project an image onto a screen so that the object distance from a lens and the image distance from a lens as well as image size can be measured. One way is to cut an arrow shape from a black piece of paper. Discard the arrow piece and secure the piece of paper with the cut-out section over the bulb end of a flashlight. Lay the flashlight on a table, with the arrow-shape opening pointing up. Lay a yardstick (meterstick) on the table so that its zero measurement is next to the covered end of the flashlight. Hold the lens at the distance from the covered end of the flashlight equal to the focal length of the lens. With the lens in this position, hold a 12-inch (30-cm)–square piece of white poster board on the opposite side of the lens from the flashlight. Move the poster board toward and away from the lens to find the distance where the sharpest image of the arrow is projected onto the poster board. Make note of the distance that the poster board is from the lens. Repeat the procedure, holding the lens at the following distances from the flashlight: (1) greater than twice the focal length; (2) twice the focal length; (3) between one and two focal lengths; (4) less than one focal length.

b. Ray diagrams can be drawn to show how an image is produced. On the diagram, show two rays coming from a point on the object: one

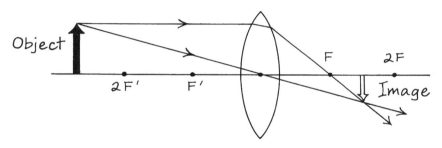

Figure 27.4

parallel to the principal axis, and a second passing through the center of the lens. The point where these two lines intersect is called the image point. For example, when the object is placed at a spot greater than twice the focal length (F), the ray diagram in Figure 27.4 indicates that the image is real, inverted, reduced, and located between F and 2F on the opposite side of the lens.

Get the Facts

1. An algebraic equation relating focal length of a lens, object distance, and image distance can be used to determine any one of the factors if the other two are known. For information about this equation, see a section on lenses in a physics text or Robert L. Lehrman, *Physics: The Easy Way* (Hauppauge, N.Y.: Barron's, 1998), pp. 451–453.

2. Light rays exiting a lens are said to be *collimated* if they emerge from the lens parallel to the principal axis and thus parallel to each other. Where must the object be to cause collimation? How are such rays used? For information, see Robert L. Lehrman, *Physics: The Easy Way* (Hauppauge, N.Y.: Barron's, 1998), pp. 445–446.

3. All convex lenses are thicker in the middle than at the edge, but all are not curved on each side, as is the double convex lens. What are the shapes of these other common convex lenses: plano-convex and concavo-convex (meniscus-convex)? Note that the water-filled lens previously made is an example of a concavo-convex lens. See a physics text for more information about lens shapes.

PART VI

Sound

28 Sound: Longitudinal Waves

If a tree falls in a forest and there is no one around to hear it, is a sound produced? The answer to this interesting question could depend on how you define sound. By the physics definition—sound is a mechanical vibration that travels through a medium—the answer is yes, sound is produced. But if you go by the physiological definition—sound is the sensation produced in hearing organs by vibrations—then no sound is produced.

In this project, you will investigate the physics definition of sound by producing sound waves and determining how the length and the material of the vibrating object affects the frequency of the sound produced. You will determine the ability of sound, which is a type of energy, to do work. You will also compare the efficiency of sound travel through the different phases of matter.

Getting Started

Purpose: To determine how the length of a vibrating material affects the frequency of sound produced.

Material
flexible plastic ruler

Procedure
1. Lay the ruler on a table so that about three-fourths of it extends past the edge of the table.
2. With one hand, keep one end of the ruler held securely to the table.
3. With the other hand, push the free end of the ruler down, then release it. Note the sound produced and how fast the free end of the ruler vibrates.
4. Repeat step 3. As the ruler vibrates, slowly move the ruler so that less of it extends over the table's edge. Note what sound the ruler makes and how fast the end of the ruler vibrates as the length of the vibrating end of the ruler decreases.

185

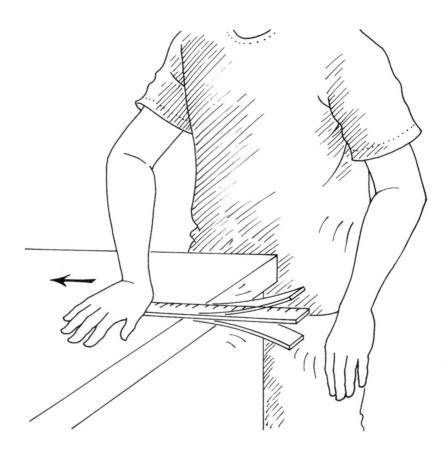

Figure 28.1

Results

As the length of the vibrating end of the ruler decreases, sound changes.

Why?

Sound is a vibration that travels through a medium. **Sound waves** are waves produced as a result of the vibration of a material. Sound originates from a vibrating object that forces the medium it passes through to vibrate. The ruler is an example of a vibrating sound source. When struck, the ruler can be observed moving back and forth at a particular **frequency** (the number of vibrations per second). The vibrations of the ruler cause the air molecules around the ruler to move back and forth at the same frequency, creating areas of **compression** (where the molecules are pushed together) and **rarefaction** (where the molecules are spread apart). Waves, such as sound waves, that have areas of compression and rarefaction are called **longitudinal waves.**

The movement of the air around the vibrating ruler transfers the sound energy through the air so that vibrating air enters your ears and hits against your eardrums, causing them to vibrate. The frequency of the vibration of the eardrums is interpreted by your brain as a specific sound called **pitch.** As the length of the ruler decreases, its frequency increases. Thus the frequency of the vibrating ruler is inversely proportional to its length. The pitch of the sound gets higher as the frequency increases.

Try New Approaches

What effect, if any, does the density of the vibrating material have on the pitch of the sound produced? Repeat the experiment using an object of comparable size but made of denser material, such as a wooden ruler.

Design Your Own Experiment

1. Sound is energy and thus is able to do work. Design an experiment to show that sound can do work by moving an object a distance. One way is to cut the bottom from a 9-ounce (270-ml) paper cup (see Figure 28.2). Use a fine-point permanent marker to draw a grid with 1-cm (or ¼-inch) squares on a 6-inch (15-cm)–square piece of waxed paper. Cover the top of the cup with the waxed paper, and secure the paper with a rubber band. Cut away any excess waxed paper. Mark an X in the center square. Lay a radio on its back so that its speaker side is up. (If speakers are separate, lay one speaker on its back.) Set the open end of the cup on the speaker. Turn the radio on to a low volume and tune it so that static is heard. You want a continuous sound with the same frequency. Determine where you should position the volume dial for low, medium, and loud volume. Turn the radio off and place one grain of rice in the center square drawn on the waxed paper (square with an X). Turn the radio onto a low volume and observe any movement of the rice grain away from the center square. Repeat the procedure using medium and loud volume. Determine the relationship between volume and sound energy.

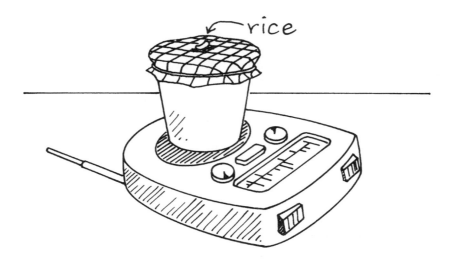

Figure 28.2

2a. Sound travels through all phases of matter—solid, liquid, and gas. Design an experiment to compare the efficiency of sound traveling through a gas and a solid. A ticking watch can be used to do this. Hold the watch at arm's length from your ear. Slowly bring the watch toward your ear until the first faint ticking sound can be heard. Measure the distance from the watch to your ear. Press your ear to a table and place the watch on the table an arm's length from your ear. Again, listen for the watch's ticking sound. If the ticking sound can be heard, ask a helper to slowly move the watch farther from your ear until the ticking sound is faint. If the ticking sound cannot be heard at arm's length, then slowly move the watch toward your ear until it can be heard. Measure the distance from the watch to your ear and compare it to the distance at which you could just hear the watch ticking through the air.

b. Design an experiment to test the efficiency of sound in water. One way would be to place the same ticking watch from experiment 2a in a sealable bag. Tie a string to the bag and lower it into an aquarium filled with water. With the watch in the center of the water at one end of the aquarium, place your ear against the aquarium at the opposite end. If the ticking can be heard, measure this distance. If not, ask a helper to move the watch toward you until the ticking can be heard, then measure this distance. Compare this distance to the distances measured in experiment 2a. For more information about sound travel in different materials, see P. Erik Gundersen, *The Handy Physics Answer Book* (Detroit: Visible Ink, 1999), pp. 213–217.

Get the Facts

1. As the temperature of air increases, its molecular motion increases. How does each degree Fahrenheit (Celsius) affect the speed of sound in air? For information, see Sir James Jeans, *Science & Music* (New York: Dover, 1968), p. 119.

2. A microphone changes sound energy into electrical energy. For information on how this is done, see Mary Jones, *Physics* (New York: Cambridge University Press, 1997), pp. 110–111.

29 Resonance: Sympathetic Vibration

As soldiers walk across a bridge, they cause the bridge to vibrate. If the soldiers march in rhythm with the natural frequency of the bridge, each step will cause the bridge to vibrate at a higher amplitude. If the amplitude is great enough, the bridge could actually collapse. This phenomenon, in which a small repeated force causes the amplitude of a vibrating object to become very large, is called resonance.

In this project, you will demonstrate sympathetic vibration, or resonance, and determine how distance affects sympathetic vibration. You will investigate how building size and stiffness affect the resonance caused by earthquakes. You will also learn how the application of a force at the same natural frequency of an object affects the amplitude of the object's motion.

Getting Started

Purpose: To demonstrate sympathetic vibration.

Materials

two identical empty 1-liter plastic soda bottles

Procedure

1. Blow across the mouth of one soda bottle to produce a constant sound. Note the pitch and the loudness of the sound.

2. As you blow across the mouth of the bottle, place the mouth of the other bottle near your ear as shown in Figure 29.1. Note any changes in the pitch and the loudness of the sound.

Results

When you blew across the mouth of the first bottle alone, you heard a sound. When you blew across the mouth of the first bottle while the second bottle was next to your ear, you heard a sound that had the same pitch as the first sound but was louder.

190

Figure 29.1

Why?

Since the two soda bottles are alike, they have the same natural frequency. Blowing across the first bottle causes the air in the bottle to vibrate, which makes the air around the bottle's mouth vibrate. This vibrating air moves outward and causes the air in the second bottle to start vibrating. Frequency is a term used in physics to denote the number of times that any regularly recurring event, such as vibrations or oscillations (swings or back-and-forth movements), occurs in one second. **Resonance** is the condition of starting or amplifying vibrations in a body at its natural vibrating frequency by an outside vibrating force having the same frequency; also called **sympathetic vibration.** Resonance occurs when the natural frequencies of two objects are the same or if one has a natural frequency that is a multiple of the other. The second bottle vibrated without air being blown across it because the vibration of the air entering it was the same frequency as the bottle's natural vibration. Since the rate of vibration for the two bottles was the same, there was constructive interference, meaning the superposition of sound waves produced a sound wave with a larger amplitude (the farthest displacement of an object from equilibrium) and thus a louder sound. The vibrating air makes a sound that you can hear when the sound waves reach your ears. So the sound waves from the two bottles together produced a louder sound but at the same pitch (how high or how low a sound is).

Try New Approaches

How does the distance of a vibrating source affect resonance? Repeat the experiment, asking a helper to hold a bottle near his or her ear while you blow across your bottle's mouth. First repeat the experiment standing about 3 feet (1 m) from your helper, then standing about 6 feet (2 m) away. Reverse positions and ask your helper to blow across the mouth of one of the bottles while you hold the other bottle near your ear.

Design Your Own Experiment

1a. An **earthquake** (the violent shaking of the earth caused by the sudden movement of rock beneath its surface) causes more resonance in some buildings than in others. Is the difference because of the size of the building? Design a way to show how size affects resonance. One way is to verify that as the circumference of paper rings decreases, the frequency at which they strongly vibrate or resonate increases. Prepare the paper strips by cutting two 1-inch (1.25-cm)–wide strips from a sheet of copy paper. One strip should be 10 inches (25 cm) long and the other 8 inches (20 cm) long. Tape the ends of each strip together to form two circular rings. Tape each ring to the center of a 4-by-4-inch (10-by-10-cm) piece of cardboard so that they are about 1 inch (2.5 cm) apart, as shown in Figure 29.2. Shake the cardboard from side to side. Start at a low frequency, by slowly moving the cardboard back and forth. Then slowly increase the frequency of your shaking by increasing the speed at which the cardboard is shaken. Notice when each of the paper rings starts to vibrate.

b. What effect does stiffness of a material have on resonance? Repeat the previous experiment, using stiff paper to make the circles.

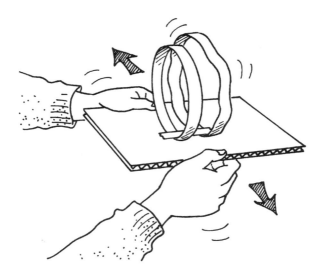

Figure 29.2

Attach the stiff circles to the ends of the cardboard used in experiment 1a so that you have the different types of paper on the same piece of cardboard. Observe the same-size rings while you shake the cardboard and determine if their frequency varies.

2a. Resonance also can be induced when a small force is applied at the right frequency. An example of this is pumping a swing. Design an experiment to demonstrate that when you apply a force at intervals close to the natural frequency of an object, the amplitude of the object will increase. Since the frequency of a pendulum depends on its length, create three or more pendulums from different lengths of string. Stretch and tie a 1-yard (1-m) string between two chairs. Tie a washer to the ends of three strings 12 inches (30 cm), 10 inches (25 cm), and 8 inches (20 cm) long. Tie the free ends of these strings about 4 inches (10 cm) apart on the horizontal string between the chairs. At regular intervals, very gently tap the side of the horizontal string near one of the chairs. Change the frequency of the tapping until one of the pendulums starts to swing. Once a pendulum starts to swing, continue tapping at this frequency for 20 swings. You can determine the frequency of the pendulum by timing the 20 swings. Then calculate the frequency using this equation:

$$F = \text{vibrations (swings)}/\text{time}$$

For example, if the time for 20 swings is 10 seconds, the frequency would be:

$$F = 20 \text{ vibrations}/10 \text{ sec}$$

$$= 2 \text{ vibrations/sec}$$

b. Determine how the movement of one pendulum can affect the movement of another pendulum with the same frequency. Tie a fourth pendulum, 12 inches (30 cm) long, on the horizontal string from the previous experiment 4 inches (10 cm) from the other 12-inch (30-cm) pendulum. Pull one of the 12-inch (30-cm) pendulums toward you and release. Observe the movement of each pendulum.

c. Does the position of pendulums of the same length affect their movement? Repeat the original experiment twice, using three pendulums, each 12 inches (30 cm) long. First tie the pendulums on the horizontal string 2 inches (5 cm) apart, then repeat by tying the pendulums 6 inches (15 cm) apart.

Get the Facts

1. A natural vibration is also called a *free vibration*. What is a forced vibration? For information, see Sir James Jeans, *Science & Music* (New York: Dover, 1968), pp. 53–54.

2. How did resonance destroy the Tacoma Narrows Bridge in Washington State on November 7, 1940? For information, see P. Erik Gundersen, *The Handy Physics Answer Book* (Detroit: Visible Ink, 1999), pp. 197–198.

PART VII

Measurement

30 | Angular Measurements: Dimensions in Degrees

Physics experiments involve the measurement of a variety of quantities. Generally we measure an object directly by placing it on or in a measuring instrument or by placing an instrument against the object. But some things are either too large, too small, or too far away to measure directly. Sizes of these objects are determined by a method called indirect measurement, which relies on mathematical calculations.

In this project, you will determine the relationship between apparent diameter (how large an object appears to be from a specific distance) and angular diameter (the apparent diameter of an object measured in radians or degrees). You will learn how to use the angular diameter of an object to indirectly measure its actual diameter. You will also learn how to construct an instrument called an astrolabe and use it to measure the angular diameter of an object. This angle will be used to calculate the actual linear diameter of an object.

Getting Started

Purpose: To demonstrate the relationship between apparent diameter and angular diameter.

Materials
masking tape
36-inch (1-m)–long strip of adding machine tape
yardstick (meterstick)

Procedure
1. Use the masking tape to secure the adding machine tape to a wall at about eye level, as shown in Figure 30.1.
2. Stand 10 feet (3 m) in front of the adding machine tape on the wall.
3. Close one eye and hold your thumb in front of the open eye.
4. Move your thumb toward and away from the wall in front of your eye until your thumb just blocks your view of the adding machine tape.

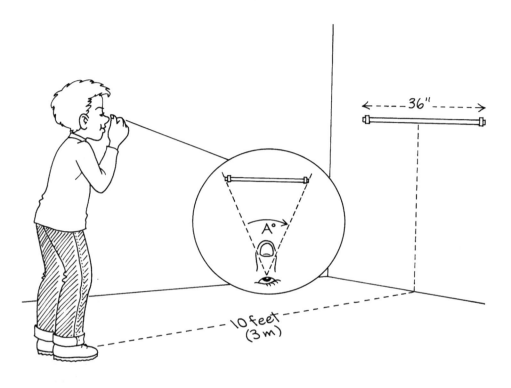

Figure 30.1

Results

At a certain distance from your eye, the width of your thumb appears to be the same size as the length of the paper strip.

Why?

It's clear when you hold the paper strip in your hand that the width of your thumb is not the same as the length of the paper strip. Your thumb and the paper only appear to be the same size when they are viewed at different distances from your eye. When your thumb and the paper are at a certain distance from your eye, they have the same **apparent diameter** (how large an object's diameter appears to be from a specific distance), so they look like they are the same size. This is because at the point where your thumb blocks the view of the paper tape, your thumb and the paper tape have the same **angular diameter** (the apparent diameter of an object expressed in degrees or radians). When two objects placed one in front of the other have the same apparent diameter, they will have the same angular diameter. In Figure 30.1, the angular diameter for the thumb and the paper strip is angle A (A°).

Try New Approaches

How does the apparent diameter of an object relate to how close or far away from the observing point it is? Repeat steps 2 through 4 of the experiment: First, while keeping your thumb in position, take four steps forward. Notice how large or how small the paper strip appears as compared to your thumb. Return to your original position. Then repeat the experiment, taking four steps backward.

Design Your Own Experiment

1. How does distance from the observer affect the angular diameter of an object? Design a way to model the affect of distance on the angular diameter of an object. One way is to draw a line across the center of a 12-inch (30-cm) square of white poster board. With a paper hole-punch, make a hole in the poster board at one end of the line. Cut three 24-inch (60-cm) pieces of string, each of a different color. Hold the strings together and fold them in half. Thread about 1 inch (2.5 cm) of the folded end of the strings through the hole in the poster board, and tape the ends to the back side (side without the line) of the poster board. Cut three 1-inch-by-6-inch (2.5-by-15-cm) strips from a sheet of colored poster board and draw a line across the center of each strip. Center the colored strips across the line on the poster board at 3 inches (7.5 cm), 6 inches (15 cm), and 9 inches (22.5 cm) from the end of the poster board with the hole. Stretch two of the same-color strings, called A_1 and A_2, across the poster board so they touch the top and bottom corners of paper strip A, as shown in Figure 30.2. Tape the strings at the edge of the poster board and cut off any excess string extending past the edge of the poster board. Repeat this procedure for the remaining strings B_1, B_2, C_1, and C_2 and paper strips B and C. Label the angles formed by the strings A°, B°, C°. This model can be displayed to represent how distance from a viewer affects the angular diameter of objects of equal sizes.

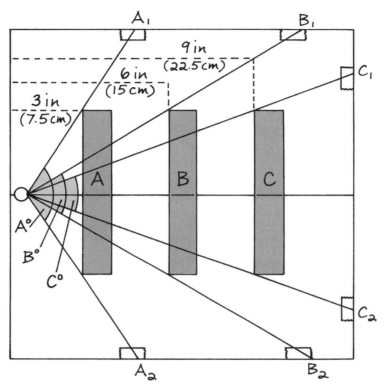

Figure 30.2

2. How can you use the angular diameter of an object to determine its
actual diameter? One way is to use the principle of similar right triangles (right triangles with the same angles but different-length
sides), which states that the tangents of similar angles of two similar
right triangles are equal. The tangent of one of the acute angles in a
right triangle is the ratio of the length of the two perpendicular lines
making up the right angle, with the side opposite the acute angle
divided by the length of the angle's adjacent side. For example, in
Figure 30.3, if the **hypotenuse** (the side of a right triangle that is
opposite the right angle) and adjacent side of angle A (∠A) for triangle CAB are extended, triangle EAD will be formed. Since the
angles of the two triangles are the same triangles, CAB and EAD are
similar right triangles; thus the tangent of one triangle is equal to the
tangent of the other.

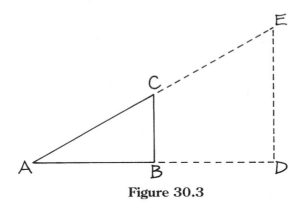

Figure 30.3

For triangle CAB: tangent ∠A = BC/AB

For triangle EAD: tangent ∠A = DE/AD

The ratio of the tangent of angle A for the two similar triangles is:

BC/AB = DE/AD

You can demonstrate this method by calculating the height of an object, such as a wall in a room. Do this by holding a 12-inch (30-cm) ruler at arm's length from your face. Record the length of the ruler, 12 inches (30 cm), as distance BC (see Figure 30.4). With the ruler extended, close one eye and look at the ruler with your open eye. Walk toward or away from the wall until the ruler's apparent height is the same as that of the wall. This means that they both appear to be the same height. Ask a helper to measure the distance from the ruler to your eye. Record this distance as AB (see Figure 30.4). Next, ask your helper to measure the distance from the wall to your eye. **CAUTION**: *For distances AB and AD, measure near but not touching your eye.* Record this distance as AD (see Figure 30.4). The ratio of the tangent of angle A for the two similar triangles is:

BC/AB = DE/AD

Thus the value of DE can be solved by using this formula:

DE = (BC × AD)/AB

For example, if BC = 12 inches (30 cm), AB = 20 inches (50 cm), and AD = 162 inches (405 cm), then:

DE = (BC × AD)/AB
DE = (12 inch × 162 inch) /20 inch
   = 97.2 inches

or in metric

$$DE = (30 \text{ cm} \times 405 \text{ cm})/50 \text{ cm}$$
$$= 243 \text{ cm}$$

Most walls in a home are 8 feet (96 inches or 240 cm) high—so either the measurement is off by 1.2 inches (3 cm) or the wall is actually 97.2 inches (243 cm) high. You could measure the wall's height to determine its true measurement and evaluate the accuracy of your measurement. Also, the example shows measurements for only one trial. Repeat the measurements four or more times at the same distance and average the results.

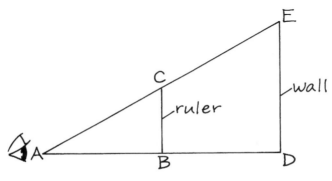

Figure 30.4

3. Angular diameter can be measured using an **astrolabe,** which is an instrument that can be used to measure **angular distances** (the apparent linear measurements between two points expressed in degrees or radians). Use the astrolabe to measure angular distances, and use it to determine the actual size of an object, such as the height of a tree.

Make an astrolabe by tying one end of a 12-inch (30-cm) piece of string through the center hole in the base of a protractor. Attach the free end of the string to a washer. Tape a drinking straw along the straight edge of the protractor. Without covering the lines, place pieces of masking tape on the protractor and write 0 to 90 on the pieces of tape (see Figure 30.5). Stand outdoors at a measured distance from a tall tree. Record this as distance AB. Ask a helper to measure from your eye to the ground, and record this as distance AD. Close one eye, and use the other eye to look through the viewing end of the straw. Sight the top of the tree through the straw. Ask a helper to read the angle where the string crosses the protractor.

Record this as angle A (∠A). Calculate the height of the section of the tree labeled BC in Figure 30.5 using this formula:

$$\text{tangent } \angle A = BC/AB$$

thus,

$$BC = \text{tangent } \angle A \times AB$$

Since AD = BE, the total height of the tree is equal to BC + AD. (See Appendix 1 for the value of tangent ∠A.)

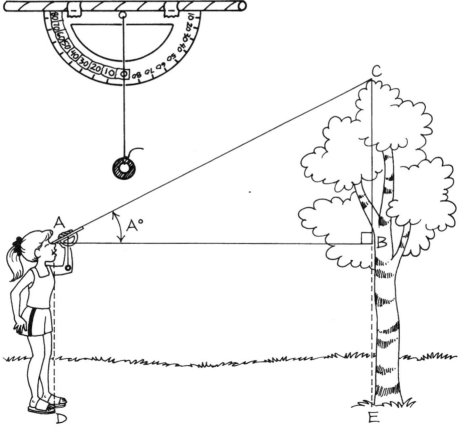

Figure 30.5

Get the Facts

During a *solar eclipse* (when the Moon moves between Earth and the Sun, thus blocking the Sun's light), the angular diameter of the Moon and the Sun are equal. During an *annular eclipse,* the Moon moves between Earth and the Sun, covering all of the Sun except a small ring around its edges. Find out more about the real and apparent diameters of the Sun and the Moon. What causes the changes in the apparent sizes of the Moon? For information, see *Janice VanCleave's A+ Projects in Astronomy* (New York: Wiley, 2002), pp. 9–15.

Appendix 1

Trigonometric Functions

Tangent Table					
Angle	cos	tan	Angle	cos	tan
0°	1.0000	.0000	45°	.7071	1.0000
1°	.9998	.0175	46°	.6947	1.0355
2°	.9994	.0349	47°	.6820	1.0724
3°	.9986	.0524	48°	.6691	1.1106
4°	.9976	.0699	49°	.6561	1.1504
5°	.9962	.0865	50°	.6428	1.1918
6°	.9945	.1051	51°	.6293	1.2349
7°	.9925	.1228	52°	.6157	1.2799
8°	.9903	.1405	53°	.6018	1.3270
9°	.9877	.1584	54°	.5878	1.3764
10°	.9848	.1763	55°	.5736	1.4281
11°	.9816	.1944	56°	.5592	1.4826
12°	.9781	.2126	57°	.5592	1.5399
13°	.9744	.2309	58°	.5299	1.6003
14°	.9703	.2493	59°	.5150	1.6643
15°	.9659	.2679	60°	.5000	1.7321
16°	.9613	.2867	61°	.4848	1.8040
17°	.9563	.3057	62°	.4695	1.8807
18°	.9511	.3249	63°	.4540	1.9626
19°	.9455	.3443	54°	.4384	2.0503
20°	.9397	.3640	65°	.4226	2.1445
21°	.9336	.3839	66°	.4067	2.2460
22°	.9272	.4040	67°	.3907	2.3559
23°	.9205	.4245	68°	.3746	2.4751
24°	.9135	.4452	69°	.3584	2.6051
25°	.9063	.4663	70°	.3420	2.7475
26°	.8988	.4877	71°	.3256	2.9042
27°	.8910	.5095	72°	.3090	3.0777
28°	.8829	.5317	73°	.2924	3.2709
29°	.8746	.5543	74°	.2756	3.4874
30°	.8660	.5774	75°	.2588	3.7321
31°	.8572	.6009	76°	.2419	4.0108
32°	.8480	.6249	77°	.2250	4.3315
33°	.8387	.6494	78°	.2079	4.7046
34°	.8290	.6745	79°	.1908	5.1446
35°	.8192	.7002	80°	.1736	5.6713
36°	.8090	.7265	81°	.1564	6.3138
37°	.7986	.7536	82°	.1392	7.1154
38°	.7880	.7813	83°	.1219	8.1443
39°	.7771	.8098	84°	.1045	9.5144
40°	.7660	.8391	85°	.0872	1.4301
41°	.7547	.8693	86°	.0698	14.3007
42°	.7431	.9004	87°	.0523	19.0811
43°	.7314	.9325	88°	.0349	28.6363
44°	.7193	.9657	89°	.0175	57.2900
45°	.7071	1.0000	90°	.0000	∞

Appendix 2

Relative Error: Percentage Error

Purpose: To calculate the relative error of experimental measurements.

Materials

calculator

Procedure

1. Calculate the average of the measurements. For example, the average of the sample experimental measurements in Table A2.1 is:

$$\text{average} = (28° + 30° + 31° + 29° + 30°) \div 5$$
$$= 29.6°$$

Table A2.1 Angles of Measurements	
Measurement	Angle, °
1	28
2	30
3	31
4	29
5	30

2. Use the following equation to determine the relative error (also called percentage error) of the measurements. For example, if the accepted (known) value for the angle measurement is 29.8°, the relative error for the experimental measurement would be:

$$E_r = E_a \div A \times 100\%$$

where E_r is the relative error, E_a is the absolute error (the difference between the known and experimental measurements), and A is the known measurement. Note that E_a is the experimental measurement minus the accepted measurement. For this sample, the absolute error is $29.6° - 29.8° = -0.2°$.

$$E_r = -0.2° \div 29.8° \times 100\%$$
$$= -0.67\%$$

The sign of the absolute or relative error merely indicates whether the result is low (–) or high (+).

Appendix 3

Manometer

Purpose: To make a manometer.

Materials

pencil

ruler

6-inch-by-30-inch (15-cm-by-75-cm)
   piece of poster board

transparent tape

scissors

9-inch (23-cm) round balloon

2-to-3-inch (5-to-7.5-cm) funnel

cup

tap water

red food coloring

spoon

48-inch (120-cm) piece of aquarium tubing

walnut-size piece of modeling
   clay

Procedure

1. Use the pencil and the ruler to mark lines across the poster board at 6 inches (15 cm) and 18 inches (45 cm) from one short side as shown in Figure A3.1.

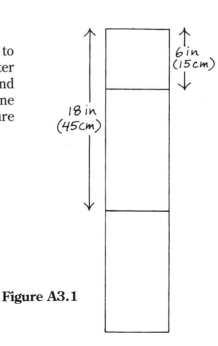

Figure A3.1

2. Fold the poster board along these lines and tape the ends together to form a three-sided stand as shown in Figure A3.2.

Figure A3.2

3. Tape the ruler vertically in the middle of one side of the stand.

4. Cut off the neck of the balloon. Discard the neck and stretch the bottom section of the balloon across the mouth of the funnel.

5. Fill the cup about one-fourth full with water.

6. Add about 20 drops of red food coloring to the cup of water. Stir.

7. Place one end of the aquarium tubing in the cup of colored water. Fill about 18 inches (45 cm) of the tube, using your mouth to suck the water into the tube as you would draw liquid into a straw. Tap the tube to release any air bubbles in the water.

8. Tape about half of the tubing to the poster board so that it forms a U shape around the ruler as shown in Figure A3.3. Note the colored water is in the U shape of the tube.

9. Insert the free end of the tubing into the end of the funnel, and seal with the modeling clay. You have made a manometer.

10. To use the manometer, place the balloon-covered funnel in an area where pressure is to be measured. A rise in the column of water on the open side of the U-tube indicates an increase in pressure.

Manometer

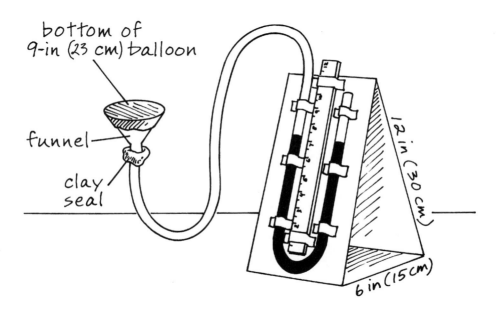

bottom of
9-in (23 cm) balloon

funnel

clay
seal

12 in (30 cm)

6 in (15 cm)

Figure A3.3

Appendix 4

Sources of Scientific Supplies

Catalog Suppliers

Carolina Biological Supply
   Company
2700 York Road
Burlington, NC 27215-3398
(800) 334-5551
www.carolina.com

Connecticut Valley Biological
   Company
82 Valley Road
P.O. Box 326
Southhampton, MA 01073
(800) 628-7748

ETA/Cuisenaire
500 Greenview Court
Vernon Hills, IL 60061
(800) 445-5985
www.etacuisenaire.com

Delta Education, Inc.
P.O. Box 3000
Nashua, NH 03061-3000
(800) 258-1302
www.deltaeducation.com

Fisher Scientific
4500 Turnberry Drive
Hanover Park, IL 60103
(800) 766-7000
www.fisherscientific.com

Frey Scientific Division of
   Beckley Cardy
P.O. Box 8101
Mansfield, OH 44903
(800) 225-3739
www.Freyscientific.com

WWR/Sargent-Welch
911 Commerce Court
Buffalo Grove, IL 60089-5229
(800) 727-4368
www.sargentwelch.com

Ward's Natural Science
5100 West Henrietta Road
Rochester, NY 14586
(800) 962-2660
www.wardsci.com

Glossary

acceleration A change in velocity per unit of time.

acceleration of free fall Free fall near Earth's surface at a constant acceleration of 32 ft/sec² (9.8 in/sec²).

adhesion The force of attraction between unlike molecules.

air The name for the mixture of gases in Earth's atmosphere.

air pressure See **atmospheric pressure.**

ammeter A device used to measure the amount of electric current in a circuit.

amp Common name for ampere.

ampere (A) An SI unit measure of electric current; also called **amp.**

amplitude The farthest displacement of an object from equilibrium.

analyzer A polarizer used to determine if light is polarized.

angle of incidence In reference to light, it is the angle between incident light and a line perpendicular to the surface it strikes.

angular diameter The apparent diameter of an object in degrees or radians.

angular distance The apparent linear measurement between two points expressed in degrees or radians.

anode A positive terminal.

apparent diameter How large an object's diameter appears to be from a specific distance.

astrolabe An instrument that can be used to measure angular distances.

atmosphere Blanket of gases surrounding a celestial body—natural objects in the sky, such as planets.

atmospheric pressure The measure of the force of air on a specific area resulting from the collision of gas molecules in Earth's atmosphere on that area; also called **barometric pressure.**

atoms The building blocks of matter.

attract To pull together.

axis An imaginary line through the center of an object and around which the object turns.

balanced forces Forces simultaneously acting on an object with the resultant force equal to zero.

barometric pressure   See **atmospheric pressure.**

battery   A device that uses chemicals to produce an electric current.

bob   For a pendulum, it is the mass attached to a string or a wire.

buoyancy   The upward force of a fluid placed on an object in it; also called **buoyant force.**

buoyant force   See **buoyancy.**

cathode   A negative terminal.

celestial bodies   Natural objects in the sky, such as planets.

center of gravity   The point where the weight of an object appears to be concentrated.

center of mass   The point at which the whole mass of an object appears to be concentrated. This is the same as the center of gravity if the object is in a uniform gravitational field, such as that about Earth.

charge   The property of particles within atoms that causes the particles to attract or repel one another or particles in other materials; also called **electric charge.**

charged   The condition of an object with more of one kind of charge than another.

charging by conduction   The process of charging a neutral body by touching it with a charged body.

closed circuit   A continuous, unbroken circuit.

coefficient of sliding friction   The ratio between the force of sliding friction between surfaces in contact with each other and the force holding the surfaces together.

coefficient of static friction   The ratio between the force of static friction between two surfaces in contact with each other and the force holding the two surfaces together.

cohesion   Attractive force between like molecules.

compression   In reference to sound waves, it is where molecules of a material are pushed together.

concave   An inward curve like the surface of a plate.

conclusion   A summary of the experimental results and a statement that addresses how the results relate to the purpose of the experiment.

conduction   See **electrical conduction** or **thermal conduction.**

conductor   A substance that is a good conductor of heat and electricity; a substance with a high concentration of free electrons; see **electrical conductor;** see **thermal conductor.**

constructive interference   The superposition of two or more waves that are in phase producing a wave of greater amplitude.

convection   The process by which heat is transferred by the movement of a fluid.

convection cell   The looping path that a convection current follows.

convection current   The rising and descending of a fluid due to differences between its density and the density of a surrounding fluid.

converge   To come together; the bending of light by a convex lens toward the lens's principal axis.

convex   An outward curve.

convexity   The measure of the outward curve of a surface.

cosine (cos)   Of an angle, equal to the length of the adjacent side divided by the hypotenuse.

coulomb (C)   The SI unit for quantity of electric charge; charge on 6.25×18^{18} electrons.

current   See **electric current.**

current electricity   Electricity due to moving electric charges.

deceleration   A decrease in velocity per unit of time; also called negative acceleration.

deflected   Turned aside.

density   A measure of the mass per volume of an object; how much matter is packed into a certain volume.

detergent   A surfactant.

diffusion   The movement of fluids due to molecular motion.

direct current (DC)   Electric current moving in one direction.

disk   A solid cylinder.

displaced   Pushed aside.

displacement   The specific distance an object is moved in a specific direction.

displacement angle   The angle the pendulum has moved from its resting position.

double convex lens   A lens that is convex on both sides; also called a double converging lens.

drag   The retarding force acting on an object moving through a fluid, such as air or water.

earthquake   The violent shaking of Earth caused by the sudden movement of rock beneath its surface.

elastic scattering   A process in which protons collide with and bounce off particles.

electrical conduction   The process by which an electrical charge moves through a material.

electrical conductivity   The measure of the ability of a substance to conduct an electric current.

electrical conductor   A substance with a high electrical conductivity; a substance with a high concentration of free electrons, such as metals.

electrical energy   Energy associated with electricity.

electrical impulse   The transfer of electrical energy from one free electron to the next due to the repulsive force between the negatively charged electrons.

electrical insulator   A material that contains a low concentration of free electrons and is a poor electrical conductor.

electric charge   See **charge.**

electric circuit   A path made of conducting materials through which an electric current travels.

electric current   The flow of electric charges through a conductor; a measure of the amount of electric charge moving through a circuit.

electric field   The property of the space around a charged object that causes forces on other charged objects.

electric force   The force between two objects due to their charges.

electricity   The name given to any effect resulting from the existence of stationary or moving electric charges.

electromagnet   A device that uses electric current to produce a concentrated magnetic field; a device made of a solenoid with a core of magnetic material, such as iron.

electromagnetic radiation   Energy transferred by electromagnetic waves.

electromagnetic spectrum   The range of wavelengths over which electromagnetic radiation extends.

electromagnetic waves   Transverse waves moving at the speed of light and consisting of rapidly alternating electric and magnetic fields at right angles to each other and to the direction in which the waves are traveling.

electromagnetism   The relationship between magnetic fields and electric currents.

electrostatic induction   The process of polarizing a neutral material (separation of positive and negative charges) due to the proximity (nearness) of a charged object.

electrons   Negatively charged particles outside the nucleus of an atom.

energy   The capacity to move something from one place to another; the ability to do work.

expand   Move farther apart, thus occupy more volume.

experimentation   The process of testing your hypothesis. Safety is of utmost importance.

filament   A thin coil of wire inside a lamp.

float   State of being suspended in or resting on the surface of a fluid.

fluid   Any liquid or gaseous material that can flow.

focal length For a lens, it is the distance from the focal point to the lens.

focal point The point at which light passing through a convex lens converges.

force A push or a pull on an object.

forced convection The use of an external device, such as a fan, to cause the transfer of heat from place to place by the movement of a fluid.

free electrons Electrons in some solids, particularly metals, that are attracted relatively equally to all nearby atoms and thus are not tightly bound to a single site and are relatively free to move through the solid.

free fall The motion of an object when the only force acting on the object is gravity. Objects falling toward Earth are said to be in free fall.

frequency The number of vibrations per second.

friction The name of forces that oppose the motion of one surface relative to another when the two surfaces are in contact with each other.

friction method The method of electrically charging neutral materials by physical contact, such as rubbing them together.

gauge A measure of a standard size, such as the circumference of a wire.

gravitational field The region of space in which a force of gravity acts on objects.

gravitational potential energy The potential energy of an object raised above an arbitrary position where the potential energy of an object is defined as zero.

gravity The force of attraction between all objects in the universe.

heat The transfer of thermal energy from one object or region to another due to differences in temperature.

hoop A hollow cylinder.

horizontally polarized In reference to light, it is a light wave whose electric field is oscillating in the horizontal direction.

hypotenuse The side of a right triangle that is opposite the right angle.

hypothesis A guess about the answer to a problem based on knowledge and research you have done before beginning a project.

image A representation of a physical object formed by a lens or a mirror.

incident light Light that strikes the surface of a material.

inclined plane A flat, slanted surface.

inertia The tendency of an object to remain at rest or to resist any change in its state of motion unless acted on by an outside force.

inertia balance An instrument that determines mass due to the periodic motion of the balance.

infrared radiation Electromagnetic radiation whose wavelengths lie just beyond the red portion of visible light; also called heat waves.

in phase In step; in reference to transverse waves, the crest of one wave would be in step with the crest of another wave.

insulator A substance that is a poor conductor of heat and electricity; a substance with a low concentration of free electrons; see **electrical insulator** or **thermal insulator.**

interference The superposition of one wave on another.

joule (J) An SI unit for work and energy.

kinetic energy (KE) The energy possessed by an object resulting from the motion of that object.

law of conservation of mechanical energy The relationship between potential mechanical energy and kinetic mechanical energy that states that the total mechanical energy of an object is equal to the sum of its potential mechanical energy and kinetic mechanical energy.

lens A curved piece of transparent material that refracts light.

liter (L) An SI unit for volume.

longitudinal waves Waves, such as sound waves, that have areas of compression and rarefaction.

machine A device that makes work easier.

macroscopic Large enough to be seen with the naked eye.

magnet A material with magnetic forces; attracts iron and other magnetic materials.

magnetic field The area around a magnet where its magnetic force can be detected.

magnetic field lines The imaginary lines making up a magnetic field that indicate the direction and magnitude of the field.

magnetic force Force produced by the motion of electric charges in a material.

magnetic north pole In reference to a magnet, it is the place where the north pole of a free-swinging magnet points.

magnetic poles The regions of a magnet where the magnetic forces appear strongest; see **north pole** and **south pole.**

magnetic south pole In reference to a magnet, it is the place where the south pole of a free-swinging magnet points.

magnetism All phenomena associated with magnets.

magnetize To cause a substance to become a magnet.

manometer An instrument used to measure the pressure of fluids.

mass The amount of matter in an object; a measure of inertia.

matter The substance of which physical objects consist; anything that takes up space and has mass.

mechanical energy (E_m) The energy of motion; the energy of an object that is moving or has the potential of moving.

mechanical stability The measure of the ability of an object to resist falling over; state of stable equilibrium.

medium Substance through which something acts.

meter (m) An SI unit for distance.

microscopic Description of a substance that is so small it requires a microscope to be seen.

momentum The value describing the amount of motion an object has.

multitester An instrument that has the ability to work like a number of instruments, including an ammeter and a voltmeter.

natural convection The movement of fluids due to difference in temperature.

net force The sum of all forces simultaneously acting on an object.

neutral Having an equal number of positive and negative charges, thus having no electric charge.

neutral equilibrium The state of an object when pushing it over does not change the height of its center of gravity.

newton (N) An SI unit for force.

Newton's third law of motion A law of motion called the law of action and reaction that relates the forces that two objects exert on each other.

north magnetic pole In reference to Earth, it is the pole near the North Pole to which the north pole of a magnet is attracted.

North Pole The northernmost point on Earth.

north pole In reference to a magnet, it is the region that is attracted to Earth's north magnetic pole; also called the magnetic north pole.

nucleus The center part of an atom.

ohm (Ω) The SI unit for electrical resistance.

Ohm's law A statement for the relationships among voltage, current, and resistance expressed by the equation $V = I \times R$, which is read: Voltage (in volts) equals the current (in amps) times resistance (ohms).

opaque Not capable of being seen through.

open circuit A circuit with a break in it so no current can flow.

optically active A material that rotates the plane of light passing through it.

oscillation To swing or move back and forth.

parallel circuit An electric circuit in which the electric current has more than one path to follow.

Pascal's law A law stating that pressure applied to an enclosed fluid is transmitted equally in all directions and to all parts of the enclosing vessel, if the fluid is incompressible.

pendulum A weight hung so that it swings about a fixed pivot; see **simple pendulum.**

period (T) The time it takes a vibrating object to complete one oscillation.

periodic motion The motion of an object, such as oscillations, that is repeated in each of a succession of equal time intervals.

photon A packet of energy consisting of a quantum of electromagnetic radiation that has both a particle and wave behavior.

pitch How high or how low a sound is.

pivot A point about which something rotates.

plane figure A geometric figure that lies on a flat surface.

polarity In reference to a magnet, it is the direction of the magnetic poles.

polarization In reference to light, refers to the direction of the electric fields in an electromagnetic wave of light.

polarization angle The angle of incidence at which light reflected from a nonmetallic surface is completely polarized.

polarized angle The best reflected angle of light for producing polarized light from a reflective surface.

polarized light Light waves with electric fields vibrating in one direction or in one plane; also called **plane polarized.**

polarizer A material that allows electric fields of light vibrating in only one direction to pass through it.

polarizing In reference to charges, it is the separation of positive and negative charges in a material with a zero net charge.

potential difference The difference in electrical potential energy between two points; measured in volts; also called **voltage.**

potential energy (PE) Stored energy; the energy of objects due to their position or condition.

pressure The measure of the force exerted on a specific area.

principal axis A line through the enter of a lens and perpendicular to its surface.

protons The positively charged particles inside the nucleus of an atom.

purpose A statement that expresses the problem or question for which you are seeking resolution.

quantum (pl., quanta) The unit of energy associated with each frequency of radiation.

radiant energy Energy that is transferred by waves and that can travel through space.

radiation The process by which hot bodies lose heat in the form of infrared radiation.

ramp An inclined plane.

rarefaction   In reference to sound waves, it is where molecules of a material are spread apart.

real image   An image formed by a lens that can be projected on a screen.

reflection   Bouncing off of.

refraction   The change of the direction of a wave as it moves from one medium to another; in reference to light, it is the bending of light as it moves from one medium to another.

repel   To push apart.

research   The process of collecting information about the topic being studied.

resistance   The measure of the opposition to flow of electric charges through a conductor.

resistor   A device used to create resistance in an electric circuit.

resonance   The condition of starting or amplifying vibrations in a body at its natural vibrating frequency by a vibrating force having the same frequency; also called **sympathetic vibration.**

restoring torque   In reference to a pendulum, it is the turning effect that reduces a pendulum's displacement angle, returning it to equilibrium.

resultant force   The single force that has the same effect as the sum of two or more forces acting simultaneously on an object.

rotation   The turning motion of an object about its axis.

rotational inertia   The property of an object that resists any change in rotational motion.

rotational kinetic energy   The kinetic energy of an object due to rotation.

rotational speed   The speed of an object rotating about its axis.

scattering   The deflection or spreading out of a beam of electromagnetic radiation as it passes through material.

scientific method   The technique of solving a scientific problem by conducting research, stating a purpose, making a hypothesis, testing the hypothesis through experimentation, and summarizing the results in a conclusion.

series circuit   An electrical circuit with only one path through which an electric current can flow.

SI   Internationally agreed-upon method of using the metric system of measurement.

simple harmonic motion (SHM)   For a simple pendulum, a condition in which the restoring torque is proportional to the displacement angle.

simple machines   The most basic machines, such as an inclined plane.

simple pendulum   A pendulum made of a bob at the end of a material, such as a string or wire of negligible mass connected to a pivot.

sliding friction   The frictional force between objects that are sliding with respect to one another.

solar energy   Electromagnetic radiation from the Sun.

solenoid   A coil of wire through which a current can pass.

sound   A vibration that travels through a medium.

sound waves   Waves produced as a result of the vibration of a material.

south magnetic pole   In reference to Earth, it is the pole near the South Pole to which the south pole of a magnet is attracted.

South Pole   The southernmost point on Earth.

south pole   In reference to a magnet, the region of a magnet attracted to Earth's south magnetic pole; also called the magnetic south pole.

space   Region without a medium.

space figure   A geometric figure that is three-dimensional.

stable equilibrium   In reference to a body at rest, it is the state of the body in which if after a slight displacement it returns to its original position; also called **mechanical stability.**

static charges   The buildup of stationary electric charges on an object.

static discharge   The loss of static charge.

static electricity   All the effects of static charges.

static equilibrium   The state of an object that is not in motion, that is at rest.

static friction   The frictional force that opposes the start of motion of an object.

superposition   Placing one thing on top of the other, such as waves.

surface tension   The cohesion between molecules in the plane of the surface of a liquid, which thus acts like an elastic skin containing the liquid.

surfactant   A substance such as a detergent that, when added to a liquid, reduces the surface tension of the liquid; also called a surface-active agent.

switch   A device used to open or close an electric circuit.

symmetrical   Having two matching halves.

sympathetic vibration   See **resonance.**

temperature   How hot or cold an object is, which is determined by the average kinetic energy of the particles of the object.

temperature gradient   The temperature change with distance along a material.

tension   Stretching force.

terminals   The points at which connections are made to an electrical device.

terminal velocity   The constant or final velocity of a falling object when the drag on it due to air resistance equals the force weight of the falling object.

thermal conduction   The transfer of heat when energetic particles collide with some of their less energetic neighboring particles; also called **conduction.**

thermal conductivity   A measure of the ability of a material to conduct heat.

thermal conductors   Materials that contain a high concentration of free electrons and are good conductors of heat; also called **conductors.**

thermal energy or **internal energy**   The sum of the kinetic and potential energy of random motion of particles making up an object.

thermal equilibrium   The state of a system in which the gain and loss of energy are equal.

thermal insulators   Materials that contain a low concentration of free electrons and conduct heat poorly.

torque   The product of a force and its perpendicular distance from a point about which it causes rotation to the axis of rotation.

translational kinetic energy   The kinetic energy of an object with translational motion.

translational motion   Motion in which the center of mass of an object moves from one place to another.

translational speed   The speed of an object being moved from one place to another.

transparent   The property of a material being so clear that it allows light to pass straight through it.

transverse waves   Waves in which the vibrations are perpendicular to the direction in which the waves are traveling; water and light waves.

unbalanced forces   Forces simultaneously acting on an object, with the resultant force not equal to zero.

uniform   The same throughout; unchanging.

unpolarized light   Light waves with electric fields vibrating in all directions.

vectors   Quantities with directions that are expressed by arrows.

velocity   Speed and direction of a moving object.

vertically polarized   In reference to light, it is a light wave whose electric field is oscillating in the vertical direction.

vibrate   To repeatedly swing or move back and forth.

vibration   See **oscillation.**

visible light   The part of the electromagnetic spectrum to which the eye is sensitive; a form of radiant energy.

voltage   Potential difference measured in volts.

voltmeter   An instrument used to measure voltage.

volts   The SI unit for potential difference; potential energy per charge.

wave   A rhythmic motion of a material or space that transfers energy from one place to another.

wavelength   The distance between corresponding points on two successive waves.

weight   The measure of the force of gravity, which on Earth is a measure of the force with which Earth's gravity pulls an object toward Earth's center.

work   What is accomplished when a force causes an object to move; the product of the force applied to an object times the distance the object moves in the direction of the force.

Index

acceleration, 41, 44, 48, 50, 213
acceleration of free fall, 50, 213
air, 50, 213
air pressure. *See* atmospheric
  pressure
ammeter:
  definition of, 116, 213
  use of, 116–117
amp, 116, 213
ampere (A), 116, 213
amplitude:
  definition of, 73, 192, 213
  pendulum, 73
  sound, 192
analyzer, 163, 213
angle of incidence, 164, 213
angular diameter, 197, 199,
  213
angular distance, 202, 213
anode, 123, 213
antenna, 167
apparent diameter, 197, 198,
  213
Archimedes, 79, 82
astrolabe:
  definition of, 202, 213
  project, 202–203
atmosphere, 50, 213
atmospheric pressure:
  definition of, 85, 87, 213
  project, 85–89
atoms, 101, 213
attract, 101, 213
axis, 60, 213

balanced forces, 44, 213
barometric pressure. *See* atmospheric pressure
battery:
  definition of, 114, 214
  in parallel, 123–124
  in series, 123–124
bob, 73, 214
buoyancy:
  definition of, 79, 82, 214
  project, 79–84
buoyant force. *See* buoyancy

cathode, 123, 214
celestial body, 50, 214
center of gravity:
  definition of, 9, 10
  projects, 9–16
center of mass, 14, 68, 214
charge, 101, 214
charged, 101, 214
charging by conduction:
  definition, 103, 214
  project, 103–104
closed circuit, 108, 214
coefficient of sliding friction, 27,
  214
coefficient of static friction, 27,
  214
cohesion:
  of water, 91
  definition of, 29, 30, 214
compression, 187, 214
concave, 91, 214

225